Traveling Entertainment in the United States

1724 - 2020

George R. Mead

ECat Worlds Press

Comments and questions? –> gmead01@gmail.com

Library of Congress Control Number: 2020911610

Mead, George R.
Traveling Entertainment in the United States 1724 - 2020

George R. Mead.
p. cm. – Traveling Entertainment in the United States
ISBN - 978-0-9890927-4-6
1. Entertainment I. Title. II. Series.

Editing by Leaf & Steel leafandsteel.com

ECat Worlds Press established its publishing program as a reaction to the large commercial publishing houses currently dominating the book industry and the smaller intellectual clones. It is interested in publishing works of fiction and non-fiction that are often deemed insufficiently profitable or commercial or that are not necessarily reflective ofcurrent literary trends and fads.

E-Cat Worlds, 57744 Foothill Road, La Grande, OR 97850
ecatworldspress [dot] com
SAN 255-6383

In the middle of nowhere - Creativity.

First Edition:
Printed in the United States of America

Fiction

From Grandeville.
Portal, 2nd edition
Lair, 2nd edition
Search
Not Again
And Again.
Magiwitch
Rebirth
Offspring
Holiday
Treasure
E'Nilt
Braidna
Seemna and Chyndra

A Tale of The Feyra
Jonathon and Dee
Dee Of The Fontala
Dee and The People
Dee and The Golden Cartouche

The Seven Lands
Seventeen Siblings (assisted by Zakke L. Zacog)

Stream
Special Investigator
Dark Souls

Non-fiction

A History of Union County
The Ethnobotany of the California Indians, 2nd Edition
A History of The Chinese in The West: 1848-1880
Yachats. The Town Called "Dark Water at the Foot of the Mountains."
The War On Poverty. A Short History - Kennedy to Reagan
A Different Look At Stress. Stress and Culture Change
Traveling Entertainment in the United States 1724 - 2020

☞ *Table of Contents* ☜

☞ *Introduction* ☜

The chapters are a series of brief histories of the various forms of Traveling Entertainment in the United States. Unfortunately there is a paucity of documentation, in any form, for the chapters dealing with anything but the circus. As you will see when pursuing the Citations, much of the information available comes in the form of web-pages which have one or two small bits of data. Some of the subject matter is sparse as no-one at that time or later made any attempt to keep records or documents, a systemic cultural problem across many things dealing with historical events in the United States. In many ways the folk of the United States live in a historical vacuum. Every once in awhile some author writes another new(?) history of P. T. Barnum or Buffalo Bill Cody. This is just intellectual carousel riding: around and around not getting anywhere. Mostly what people, authors, newspapers, etc., write about, are celebrities and frequently provide little information other than a fascination about the individuals behavior, often in a non-historical temporal dimension. This is reflected in the limited documentation in the several chapters. Over and over and over again one sees the same information repeated in book after book, frequently almost verbatim. Often what does get written about is when the behavior being discussed ran contrary to the cultural norms of the time. As an example of how much work needs to be done when writing neglected history, Norman Anderson began in 1980 developing his "Ferris Wheels: An Illustrated History." It was published in 1992.

One further point. In various of the chapters the following terms are used: Indian, colored, and Negro. These are the terms used in various pieces of the information found during the writing of this bit of history. The PC folk probably think these terms ought to be changed into such terms as Native America, or African American. Ones does not rewrite historical commentary to satisfy modern concepts of proper nomenclature which is in itself ever changing.

☞ Once Upon A Time ✌

(a wee look at some cultural values/beliefs)

Benjamin Lundy was born in 4 January 1789 to Joseph and Elizabeth Shotwell Lundy, both Quakers, at Greensville, Hardwick Township, Sussex County, New Jersey.

Benjamin Lundy brought his newspaper, *Genius of Universal Emancipation*, to Baltimore, Maryland, in 1825. It was started in January 1821 while he was living in Mount Pleasant, Ohio. It was now, in 1825, a weekly newspaper that stressed the emancipation of all slaves.

William Lloyd Garrison, born 10 December 1805, in Newburyport, Massachusetts, became a prominent American abolitionist, journalist, suffragist, and social reformer. He was one of the founders of the American Anti-Slavery Society. He promoted "immediate emancipation" of slaves in the United States.

Lundy was joined by William Lloyd Garrison, who started as a writer and co-editor of Lundy's newspaper in September 1829. Harrison was focused on immediate and complete emancipation while Lundy favored a more gradualist approach including finding a homeland abroad for the free slaves. Harrison eventually became a traveling speaker against slavery.

The size of the population of the colonies that later became the United States increased steadily in the decades prior to, and including, the American revolution. The first decennial census, mandated in the U.S. Constitution, took place in 1790. Since that time, the natural increase, i.e. the excess of births over deaths, has been a constant contributor to population growth. The other factor, immigration, has ranged from negligible to large at various points in the nation's history. The tendency in agricultural economies for early marriage and large numbers of children resulted in regular population growth during the decades preceding 1830, with only a small contribution from immigration.

In 1831, Garrison, with Isaac Knapp, founded an abolitionist newspaper, *The Liberator*, which was published in Boston until slavery was abolished by Constitutional amendment in 1865.

Its circulation was quite small, around 3,000 subscribers, three-quarters were African-American.

The American Civil War ran from 1861 to 1865 after 7 southern states declared that they had seceded from the 34 states then in existence. The Confederacy collapsed, slavery was abolished, and four million slaves were freed, with much of the South's infrastructure destroyed. The destruction heavily impacted the transportation system in the south.

In July 1865, *The Nation*, founded in New York City by Joseph H. Richards, became a successor to *The Liberator*. It was focused on matters of concern and the interests of its small but influential audience, often described as reform-minded Protestant elites.

Barnum's Museum burned down in July 1865.

Two weeks after the museum fire, *The Nation* printed, on 22 July 1865, an unsigned article which stated:

Barnum's Museum is gone at last.

The more one aspires to neatness, exactness, and care in his own private "cabinet," the more he will revolt at slovenliness, in a large and more public museum.

We desire to give the late "American Museum" all the credit

it deserves. For it needs it all. Its memory is not pleasant. It pandered to the most foolish curiosity and to the most morbid appetite for the marvelous.

The British Museum is a national institution, founded and supported by the revenues and the government of an empire. The American Museum of the future will be such another, and even more worthily lodged.

But of one thing let us be certain. No individual or stock company may undertake to form and manage a museum by way of making money will be of any great or permanent service to the community.

In a letter *To The Editor Of The Nation*, on 29 July1865, printed August 10, Barnum wrote a response (emphasis, etc. in original):

THE NATION is just the journal *our* "nation" needed, and it delights thousands beside my humble self. But the article on "Museums" in the last number exhibits a little of the slashing style of the *London Saturday Review*, or else I am blinded by my prejudices or interests.

Humbug with me has had its day, and although I always gave the money's worth of that which was *not* demoralizing, I often grieved that the taste of the million was not elevated.

If I build another museum, it will be fire proof . . .

I hope that the fire of the late museum will have fumigated and burned out the humbug from the public mind to such a degree that it can discover that Barnum has got neither horns nor hoofs, and that he has as much love for refinement and the elevation of the race, especially in this country, as even your excellent writer, "or any other man."

However, the new museum burned to the ground in 1868.

After that Barnum retired from the museum business.

All of the above sets the stage, so to speak, as the various cultures discussed in the following chapters developed.

☞ The Circus Comes to Town ✎

There are more than 1,250 books written in English about the circus (Culhane 1991).

This is a brief history of *circus* in the United States. Chindahl (1959) wrote:

> Of the three types of exhibitions, the menagerie is the oldest. It has its beginnings prior to the American Revolution when colonial settlement in what is the United States was confined to a strip about one hundred and fifty miles wide along the Atlantic coast.

> There were no zoological gardens or other permanent located collections of animals in America at that time, and indeed until long after, a tropical animal was a great curiosity, and the news that a living lion or tiger could be seen at the local inn created much interest.

Vail (1933) wrote [spelling as written]:

> It is probable that strolling acrobats and clowns travelled through the colonies at a very early period, or at least through all of them except New England where their presence was

without doubt discouraged by parson and beadle. A troup reached Philadelphia as early as 1724, however, and their advertisement in the "American Weekly Mercury" of May 7th gives us a good picture of them and their show. As we read the announcement we realize how little this type of performance has changed from Elizabethan times to the present and it is particularly interesting that the spectators were allowed to sit on the stage, just as in the days of Shakespeare.

West (1981) wrote that:

Americans were watching multi-act circus performances as early as the 1790's: however, it was not until the 1820's and '30's that attending circuses became a significant national pastime. It is important to note, though, that the rise in the popularity of circuses occurred while the nation was experiencing a revival of puritanical values. The religious, political, and educational leaders of the 1820's, '30's, and '40's were quick to denounce nearly all forms of commercial amusements and diversions. The only types of recreational activities which were above reproach were those that were of an educational or religious nature, such as attending lectures or church functions. Hence, it is not surprising that the circus, along with the stage and the concert-hall, was often subject to criticism and public condemnation. When the circus came to town, it was common for the local clergy to forbid their congregations to attend the circus performances.

Animals on displayed were: 1716 - "Lyon of Barbary;" 1721 - a camel; 1733 - a polar bear; 1768 - a leopard (Chindahl 1959).

The announcement of the first lion on exhibition was in Boston in 1716 (Vail 1945):

> To be shown by William Nicholas at the house of Captain Arthur Savage in Brattle Street, a Lyon of Barbary, with many other rarities, the like never before seen in America.

Vail (1933) wrote [spelling as written]:

> It is appropriate that the king of beasts should lead the procession which was eventually to find its way to the menagerie and the circus. His first appearance {Vail's later article updated the early date] in this country is described as follows in the "Boston Gazette" of September 26, 1720: The lyon being the King of Beasts, and the only one of his kind in America is removed from Capt. Arthur Savages, to Mrs. Martha Adams's at the South End of Boston, where attendance will be constantly given, (while he remains in this country,) to any person or persons who has the curiosity to see the same.

> This advertisement appeared from time to time until July 3, 1721, when a new announcement appeared as follows:

> At the South End of Boston, at the house of Mrs. Adam's is to be seen the Lyon, where on a sign is writ these words. The Lion King of Beasts is to be seen here. He is not only the largest and most noble, but the tamest and

most beautiful creature of his kind, that has been seen, he grows daily, and is the wonder of all that see him: Constant attendance is given to all persons who desire to satisfy themselves with the sight of him.

In England a number of prominent riding schools were established by 1760. Philip Astley and his wife demonstrated horsemanship in the Halfpennny Hatch field on the south bank of the Thames River. The forty-two foot diameter ring was probably determined, by Astley in 1768, as the smallest size for a circling horse. He had found that when a trained horse cantered around a circle of that size with the horse and rider leaning just a little toward the center of the ring that centrifugal force would keep the rider in balance. One of his horsemen, Charles Hughes, in 1782 opened his own school, *The Royal Circus,* on the Blackfriars Road, which was apparently the first time in relatively modern times that the term "circus" was used (Hoh and Rough 1990, Culhane 1991, Johnson 1990).

The early circuses in the United States were rather small, being mainly equestrian exhibitions. Chindahl (1959) suggested:

> The American circus grew up during a period when most men rode horseback and, occasionally, if not frequently, harnessed and drove horses. In those days a beautiful, well-trained horse was an object of critical admiration. No wonder, then, that horsemanship was the essential and characteristic feature of the circus during its formative period.

In 1771 the Philadelphia newspaper ran an advertisement for Mr. Faulks who performed "feats in horsemanship." In that same year John Sharp, from England did the same thing. The next year, 1772, Jacob Bates gave what he called "a burlesque on horsemanship, or The Taylor riding to Brentford." And in August 1785, Thomas Pool, did much the same thing with the addition of a clown and several musicians to add to the entertainment. Pool had a trick horse that could lie down and groan, "then sit up like a lady's lap-dog, then rise to his feet and make his manners to the ladies and gentlemen" (Chindahl 1959, Culhane 1991, Vail 1933).

The circus began to develop in America as animal acts at fairs or taverns, the Clown in harlequinades, originally a silent act with music and stylized dance, employing some dialogue as singers and joke tellers, but primarily a visual spectacle, with the showy maneuvers of horsemen as the main portion of the show.

A menagerie show on 26 December 1781 advertised itself as an: "Exhibition of the most beautiful, curious and extraordinary productions of nature, ever exposed to view in America" and consisted of "birds, reptiles, snakes and quadrupeds" (Vail 1933).

Bogdan (1988) suggested that:

> Elephants, giraffes, orangutans, and many of the human oddities that were exhibited were simply out of the realm of eighteenth- and early-nineteenth American's experience.

In 1786 Charles Willson Peale founded the *"Respository for Natural Curiosities,"* or, *Philadelphia Museum,* situated in the Long Room of the Pennsylvania State House. Later he opened a museum, *Peale's Museum,* on the second floor of

Independence Hall in Philadelphia, Pennsylvania, that offered art, music, history, and nature (fossils; preserved animals, birds, and insects; the skeleton of a mastodon) as well as scientific and industrial inventions, with a few oddities.

Brigham (1996) wrote, in describing the museum, that:

> Peale gradually reoriented this electric exhibition to exemplify two hierarchical schemes, the Linnaen classification of species and the Great Chain of Being. Application of the first helped Peale gain credibility within the scientific community, while the second furthered Peale's interest in present a view of the animal kingdom and society as rank-ordered yet independent.
>
> On the walls of the museum, Peale inscribed quotations to inspire Christian contemplation of divine works in nature. His lectures and advertisements quoted directly from biblical passage, and he actively sought the support of Philadelphia's clergymen in promoting the museum. Many of them endorsed the museum's teachings, and they consistently argued that there was no contradiction between scientific knowledge and Christian piety.

The Great Chain of Being, or *scala naturae*, was derived from the classical and medieval concept of the proper order of the universe as a fixed state of organization. Everything in that system was held in a strict hierarchical system from the most base rock at the bottom of the chain up to the Prime Mover, God, at the top, and beneath him, the angels, existing in the form of spirits.

Every link in the chain, starting at the bottom, added a positive attribute to the one above. In this system, rock possesses existence, plants possess existence and life, beasts (animals) possess existence, life, motion, and appetite. Man, of course, held a special place in this system as possessing mortal flesh with all the attributes of the beasts as well as of the spirit. The desires of the flesh could drag one down, while the way of the spirit is higher and noble. The struggle between flesh and spirit was considered as a moral one.

Everything in the chain was divided and subdivided in order to account for all that one could see in existence. Everything fit somewhere, giving meaning and order to life and existence. This system of understanding was locked tightly to the current religious thought and the concept of original creation.

In 1792 John Bill Ricketts, an English teacher of horsemanship, emigrated from Britain, to establish a circus, in Philadelphia where he built *Ricketts' Art Pantheon and Amphitheatre,* in which he conducted a riding school. He had trained as an apprentice in England from 1772-1793 with the Scotsman Charles Huges. On 3 April 1793, he gave circus performances, a series of equestrian exhibitions two to three times a week. He combined equestrians, acrobats, trained animals and clowns. Ricketts advertised [spelling as written] in New York City that his show had added to its attractions: "The Indian Chiefs, lately arrived, will with Mr. Ricketts, perform on horseback, drest in the character of warriors." This predated the much later shows such as *Buffalo Bill's Wild West Show.*

George Washington, who had visited the show, on 22 April 1793, and 24 January 1797, became good friends with

Ricketts, with the two taking recreational rides together.

In 1795 Ricketts hired Matthew Sully, a prominent English singer, acrobat and clown from Sadler's Wells Theatre in London. He hired also John Durang, considered to be the first American-born circus clown, as a member of the troupe beginning in October 1796. Washington sold his horse to Ricketts for $150. The program by 1796 had riding, tightrope dancing, ground and lofty tumbling, clowning, and pantomime. The show toured Canada in the summer of 1797 and later in the year President John Adams visited the circus. Ricketts mixed equestrian acts with clowning alternated with harlequinades (the part of a pantomime that featured a mute character with goofing around with a clown) and *Stage Performances*. The circus also included ballets. The small troupe toured South Carolina, Virginia, Maryland, and New England (Chindahl 1959, Hoh and Rough, 1990, Culhane 1991, Vail 1933).

Hoh and Rough (1990) wrote that:

> In the first half-century following 1793 . . . Americans moved rapidly westward. Within thirty years, there were several small but significant circuses touring the new world with two or three wagons, some horses, and a clown. Early circus troopers had to be a rugged bunch of pioneers: roads west were little more than widened trails when the first circus wagons challenged them.

Chindahl (1959) listed the states that came into being with the westward movement of people and the change in frontier life as the immediate western edge of settlement shifted away from the east coast: Kentucky, 1792; Tennessee,

1796; Ohio, 1802; Louisianan, 1812; Mississippi, 1817, Illinois, 1818; and, Alabama 1819. He points out that traveling west during these times was by blazed trails that were more suitable for horsemen, pack animals, than for wagons.

In 1796 the first elephant entered the North American continent on 13 April, noted in the publication, *Greenleaf's New York* , which mentioned a two-year old (often stated as a three-year old) female elephant journeying to our shores aboard ship. A few days later an elephant was exhibited around Beaver Street and Broadway, according to an advertisement in *The Argus* on 23 April 1796. The animal was owned at first by Captain Jacob Crowninshield, of the ship, *America*, and was known as "Crowninshield's elephant." In his journal, dated 2 November 1795, Crowninshield wrote:

> We take home a fine young elephant two years old, at $450.00. It is almost as large as a very large ox, and I dare say we shall get it home safe, if so it will bring at least $5000.00. We shall at first be obliged to keep it in the southern states until it becomes hardened to the climate.

The Crowninshield family operated a shipping business out of Salem, Massachusetts (Kelly n.d., Hoh and Rough 1990, Culhane 1991).

The ketch *America* was the second ship bought and sold by their business. It was first named *John*, one of the two large ketches built at Salem in 1794, for Elias Hasket Derby for use in the foreign trade. After being purchased by the family in 1874 it was insured by Crowninshield in March 1975, and sent on a trip to Calcutta. It was probably sold in the early summer after returning from that trip

(Goodwin1925, Williams 2009, Hitchings and Phillips 1906). A ketch has two masts with the mizzen mast stepped before the rudder head. The mizzen sail in a ketch is a driving sail, often much smaller than the mainsail.

The female elephant was sold in New York City for $10,000 to Owen, a Welshman from Philadelphia who moved her to that town for exhibition. A handbill, dated 27 June 1797, stated where the elephant could be viewed: " A place is fitted up for him (suitable to receive genteel Company), in a store back of the Coffee House where he will remain til the 8th of July only, as he is to be a Cambridge at the approaching commencement. Admittance, One Quarter of a Dollar – Children, One Eight of a Dollar" (Vail 1945).

The *Lailson and Jaymond's Circus* arrived in New York City in December 1797 and constructed a new building in which to present "a grande display of Horsemanship" (Poppiti 2018).

In early 1800 Ricketts sold his goods and sailed for England; the ship foundered and he drowned (York County History Center 2015, Culhane 1991).

In 1808 Hackaliah Bailey of Stephentown (later known as Somers), Westchester County, New York, purchased an Indian elephant he named *Old Bet,* or *Little Bet,* the second brought to America, arriving into Boston harbor in 1804 (or 1805 as some reported). Bailey traveled with a trained dog, several pigs, a horse and four wagons which formed the *Bailey Circus,* renting barns as exhibition halls. Jensen (1975) wrote that Hachaliah had bought the elephant from his brother, a sea captain, in 1815, who had bought it at auction in London for $20.00 and sold it to his brother for $1,000. The circus traveled by night, showing by day in barnyards and tavern courtyards, charging twenty-five cents admission. In that same year he sold "for $1200, equal two-thirds use of an elephant for one year" to Andrew Brown and Benjamin Lent (Vail 1933, Hoh and Rough 1990).

"Two Tigers from Surat" were exhibited at Crombie's Tavern in Salem on 7 July 1806. In 1806 there was an advertisement for the two royal *tygers* "at Mr. Brevoort's, 26 Chatham Street, New York, one of which was called 'the Royal Tyger Nero.' "

Pepin and Breschard, an equestrian group, arrived in New York City from Madrid, Spain, in November 1807. The show owned by a American, Victor Pepin, and a Frenchman, Jean Bapiste Casmier Breschard. Victor Pépin, was one of Rickett's students. The Circus of Pépin, Breschard and Mariotini was the first to bring a circus west of the Appalachian Mountains to such frontier cities as Pittsburgh, Pennsylvania. Their circus moved west to Cincinnati, Ohio in 1814. They advertised their premier in New York City as the "First professors of the art of riding and agility on horseback." In 1810 it was the first show of its kind to visit Boston. It had to set up the show in Charlestown, outside of Boston city limits, as such performances were prohibited inside Boston City limits. Pepin's circus disbanded in 1829 in Nashville (Vail 1933, Culhane 1991, Wall 2013, 19thCenturyLives 2013a, 19thCenturyLives 2013b, Brown 1994).

They had built theaters in New York City; New Orleans; Charlestown, Massachusetts; Baltimore, Maryland; Richmond, Virginia; Alexandria, Virginia; Charleston, South Carolina; and Pittsburgh and Philadelphia, Pennsylvania, while touring until 1815.

During this time the word "circus" tended to label the building where the performance was held rather than the troupe performing in it (Hoh 2004). American cities did not have the population base to support the development of circuses only inside relatively permanent buildings such as those in New York, so the circuses rapidly developed into road shows (Hoh and Rough 1990).

There were at least two elephants touring in 1806, one named "Bet," the other "Little Bet." Both were killed by local folk. "Bet" was killed by an irate farmer, Daniel Davis, in Alfred, Maine, where he operated a sawmill. He apparently saw the elephant as the real-life incarnation of the Biblical "behemoth" and felt that it was some sort of sinful thing to exhibit such a thing, or, perhaps he may have simply been drunk (his reason is unclear in the reporting). He fired two musket shots and killed the elephant. She died on the side of the road. Davis spent two days in jail for his crime (American Heritage 1974, Hoh and Rough 1990). A newspaper article stated that "Bet" was killed in the town of Berwick when passing from Boston to the District of Maine (Culhane 1991).

"Little Bet" was killed by six adolescent boys on 25 May 1826, on the bridge over the Chepachet River, in Chepachet, Rhode Island. They apparently were testing a boast made at a performance that the elephant's hide was so thick that no bullet could pierce it. The boys' fathers had to pay $1,500 to the irate owners of the elephant (Hoh and Rough 1990, Vail 1933).

Bailey's success stimulated a number of folk from Westchester, Putnam, and Duchess counties to do similar things: Thadeus, Jerimiah, and Gerard Crane; Caleb S. Angevine; John J. June; Lewis B. Titus; Benjamin and Lewis Lent; and, members of the Brown, Purdy, Wright, Finch, and Ganung families (Chindahl 1959, Somers Historical Society n.d., Culhane 1991).

Bailey bought "Nero, the Royal Tiger, and Cage," for $1,000 from Benjamin Lent in December 1809. It was also stated that four days later Bailey traded "One quarter of the earnings of an elephant for the purchase of one quarter of Lent's tiger" which raises the unanswerable question as to what was really going on? (Culhane 1991, Vail 1933).

John Scudder purchased, in 1809, a collection of various items from various owners and founded the *American Museum* in 1810. The museum displayed objects that people would not normally see. Some things on display were live; others were skeletal recreations; some were fabrications of things that may or may not have actually existed. It held "The Original Flag" of 1788 that had been hoisted on top of a battery by the America forces. This flag was to stay there as long as the institution existed (Greenwood 2015).

Cayeto, Codet, Menial, and Redon had an equestrian "circus" in 1810 in Boston and later in 1812 opened in a building called the "New York Circus" (Greenwood 2015).

P. T. Barnum was born on 5 July 1810, in Bethel Village, an unincorporated section of Danbury Connecticut, the first child of Philo Barnum's second wife, Irena Taylor. His father had been one of the five men who had been the founders of the village (Kunhardt et al 1995).

Traveling menageries began to develop in 1813. The area around Somers, New York, rapidly developed into a center for entrepreneurs of the traveling menageries whose animals lived in local farmer's barns (Hoh and Rough 1990).

Menageries were essentially traveling mini-zoos at which the customers could stand and stare at the animals.

Hackaliah Bailey hired the teenaged Nathan Howes to tour, in 1816, with the *Nathan Howes Menagerie* for a fifty-fifty split in profits. Howes apparently didn't do that until Bailey stated that he was going to shoot his half of the elephant (Culhane 1991).

Later Hackaliah Bailey worked for P.T. Barnum after he had visited Barnum's store in Bethel, Connecticut (Ariano 2004).

Vail (1933) wrote [spelling as written]:

> From the earliest times the circus has had to fight against prejudice. At one time it was quite generally thought that circuses, like gypsies, recruited their ranks by stealing children, and the clergy generally opposed them at every turn. An early attack, which incidentaly mentions one of the first circuses to venture into the pioneer west, appeared in the Chillicothe, Ohio "Weekly Recorder" for August 2,1815:

The article quoted in the above clip stated that:

> The principal object pursued by the conductors of the Circus is to enrich themselves at the expense of others. How far they have succeeded in their design in this place—what number of citizens have honoured them with their presence, and favoured them with their support, we have not been particularly informed. Believing that these men are prosecuting an unlawful calling—one that cannot be defended on Scriptural ground, or on principles of sound reason and good policy, we presume that the good sense of the citizens in general would lead them to treat their exhibitions with that unqualified neglect and contempt which they so justly deserve. . . .
> The situation of our country demands the consideration of all good citizens. It is infested

with dishonest, unprincipled men of various
descriptions — swindlers, counterfeiters,
stageplayers, show men, etc. . . .

Mr. Vilalliave's traveling company, the *New York Circus*, opened 30 June 1814, in New York City, with an organization of male and female acrobats only. They did rope dancing, tumbling, and pyramid building while some sang songs or did pantomime (Vail 1933).

In 1820 there are about thirty circuses, called rolling shows, traveling around New England and the Atlantic States. These were, typically, a couple of wagons, four horses, and half a dozen performers (a clown and a few tumblers and vaulters) (Greenwood 2015). There were, around the same time, about thirty traveling menageries (Culhane 1991).

June, Titus, and Angevine toured, in 1820, their menagerie of sixty wagons, with Isaac A. Van Ambough, dressed in a Roman toga, as caretaker (Culhane 1991, Vail 1933).

A newspaper advertisement from 19 September 1820 was headed "An Exhibit of two great natural Curiosities. An elephant and the African Lion" (Chidahl 1959).

James Hunter, from Astley's Amphitheatre in London, joined with Price and Simpson after they sent their show to Philadelphia where the advertisements stated he rode "a horse in a rude state of nature," that is, he rode bareback. Before this the equestrians utilized saddles or pads. Another performance done by riders was to jump over a banner, and then the rider would jump from his horse through a balloon held out by another or fastened to a pole. It was considered a big feat. The "balloon" was a hoop eighteen inches in diameter covered with paper (Vail 1933, Wittmann 2012).

The number of circuses that were advertising over the next five years was: 1823, five; 1824, five; 1825, nine; 1826, thirteen; 1827, twelve; 1828, sixteen (Thayer 2005).

In 1825, Joshuah Purdy Brown, from the region of Somers, New York, replaced the usual wooden construction with a full canvas tent in which he started a one ring show with a few hundred seats. Nathan Howes ordered a tailor-made tent the following year. By the mid-1830s the tent became commonplace (Thayer 2005, Journal News 1984). Brown utilized a thirty-six foot, umbrella-shaped sailcloth tent, stating that this was a "Pavilion Circus" (Wall 2013, Culhane 1991).

Tents opened up new markets as the circus could put on shows in locales that did not have big enough permanent buildings within which the circus could operate. They became the solution to guarantee a protection from the climate for the audiences as well as a consistent set-up for the acts (Wall 2013, Hoh and Rough 1990).

After Brown toured Delaware he went into Virginia, the Mississippi Valley, Natchez, and New Orleans (Wall 2013).

In 1826, Aaron Tuner, Nathan Howes, Sylvester Reynolds started, 1828, their circus, *The Columbian Circus*. It was based in Danbury and tended to only tour through New England. He utilized a tent, ninety feet in diameter, made from Russian duck, a white linen canvas (Wall 2013, Culhane 1991). Turner operated circuses 1820-1850 either as a sole owner or in partnership. Some of these partners were Nathan A. Howes, Lewis B. June, and George F. Bailey (Turner's son-inlaw). His earlier circus probably consisted of six people (three were boys), two to three horses, no menagerie, and a ring curb. The show could have been transported by stagecoach and the regular freight wagons. Bailey eventually took over the operation of the circus and enlarged it. Bailey later became P.T. Barnum's right-hand man and remained in the circus business until 1875 (Chindahl 1959).

P. T. Barnum opened in February 1828, a store in Bethel, Connecticut. In 1829 he married Charity Hallett. He was 21; she was 19. The store ran from 1828 to 1833 (Culhane 1991).

In Philadelphia the menagerie of Raymond and Waring displayed their animals in a building they had erected on Walnut above Eight. They sold everything to "General" Rufus Welch and Lewis B. Lent, then Welch solely owned it, then he partnered with Titus, June, and Angevine. For a time Van Amburgh and his caged cats traveled with the Welch and Bartlett show, ca. 1829-1830 (Vail 1933).

On 19 April, 1829 a circus company was charged by Sunbury, Pennsylvania, with witchcraft after their performance (Johnson 1990).

The first rhinoceros, probably an Indian rhinoceros, labeled "The Unicorn, or One Horned Rhinoceros," landed in Boston on 3 May 1830. It was shown by the *June, Titus, and Angevin* menagerie as part of the *American National Caravan* (Rookmaaker 1998).

J. Purdy Browen, a cousin of Hackaliah Bailey, toured his menagerie and circus together in 1823. It was the first time this had happened (Hoh and Rough 1990).

Chindahl (1959) cites an advertisement in a Tallahassee newspaper [probably the Floridian and Advocate which ran 1831-1842] issued on 14 February 1832 promoting "A Grande Menagerie of Living Animals" to be seen beginning on 16 February.

Tippo Sultan, the great hunting elephant, the tiger of Brazil, the camel of Arabia imported in1830, the cougar of South America, two panthers of North America, a prairie wolf, an ichneumon of Egypt, together with a great variety of the monkey tribe; also Dandy Jack, the celebrated equestrian, who will perform many interesting and diverting feats on his much admired Shetland pony. Good music during the performance.

In 1833, a structure was built in New York City to be the site for both menagerie and circus performances. It was converted in 1835 into an amphitheater with a stage and a circus ring, and named the *Bowery Amphitheatre* (Brown 2018).

Issac A. Van Amburgh was a caretaker and animal trainer of animals in the *Van Amburgh Menagerie*. In 1833, he changed from just showing the animals to stepping into the cage and demonstrating his animal trainer capabilities. There was no attempt to show performing animals, it was enough amazement for the audiences to see a man step into a cage with them (Vail 1933, Culhane 1991). This was the beginning of animal acts for circus shows.

The first time Van Amburgh stepped into the cage on the stage of the Richmond Hill Theatre, New York, 1833, his biographer, O. J. Ferguson, wrote (Culhane 1991):

The effect of his power was instantaneous. The Lion halted and stood transfixed. The Tiger crouched. The Panther with a suppressed growl sprang back, while the Leopard receded gradually from its master. The spectators were over-whelmed with wonder ... Then came the most effective tableaux of all. Van Amburgh

> with his strong will bade them to come to him
> while he reclined in the back of the cage – the
> proud King of animal creation.

What his biographer didn't mention was how extremely abusive Van Amburgh was with his animals. He beat them into submission and often starved them for three days before a performance. It certainly didn't have anything to do with some mystical "will power," which was a form of humbug (Hoh and Rough 1990, Johnson 1990, Brooke 2001).

Lewis Lent, of Somers, New York, in 1834 invested in *J.R. & W. Howe, Jr., & Co.* menagerie (of North Salem), purchasing a half interest in their menagerie of a rhinoceros, a polar bear, a leopard, and cages. He joined in 1835 the *Brown & Co.* circus and became a partner in 1836 (Somers Historical Society N.D.).

A lion and two Arabian horses were given to President Andrew Jackson by the Emperor of Morocco in 1834. In 1835, the President asked Congress what to do with them. They advised selling them. In an auction in Washington D. C, the lion was purchased by an agent for a menagerie for $3,350, proceeds to be given to three local orphan asylums (Vail 1933). It was probably the June, Titus, and Angevine menagerie.

Two circuses traveled in the south in 1834: *Sizer's Circus*, and the *French, Hobby and Company's Baltimore Menagerie and Circus.* Sizer's Circus, a small circus, began in 1833, and traveled in the south. The other was formed by J. E. W. Hobby in 1834 although it seems he had acquired some, or all, of "A Grande Menagerie of Living Animals" noted above in the year 1833 (Kotar and Gessler 2011, Slout 2010).

Sizer's Circus advertised that it would be in Talahassee

on December 18 1834 (Chindahl 1959):

> Grand entry of six horses, sports of the ring by the whole company; comic song by the clown; exhibitions of horsemanship and still vaulting; equestrian exercises by Mrs. Sizer, the intrepid female equestrian. Comic duet, "Polly Hopkins and Tommy Tompkins," by Mrs. Sizer and Mr. Gullens, The whole to conclude with the laughable scene of "Billy Button's Unfortunate Journey to Brentford . . . " Permanent seats for ladies. No smoking.

The French, Hobby and Company's Baltimore Menagerie and Circus advertised on 27 December 1834 that it would be in Tallahassee on 12 January 1835 (Chindahl 1959):

> Elephant, camel, lion, leopard, tiger, hyena, kangaroo, panther, black bear, armadillo, emew, swan, catamunda, ichneumon, large number of apes, monkeys, and baboons. Dandy Jack and his pony. Animals exhibited one hour, then equestrian performance. Band. Comic song by clown. Seats for 500 to 600 . . . will exhibit in Marianna, Jan. 7; Mt. Vernon, Jan. 9; Quincy, Jan. 10.

Until 1835 Philadelphia had been America's largest city. Then New York City began to grow due to its trans-Atlantic shipping ties. In 1835, the farm population was still larger than the urban population. New York City developed as a circus town with a number of permanent structures built to support them (Hoh and Rough 1990).

The menagerie men of Westchester and Putnam Counties of New York came to dominate the outdoor exhibition business in the northeast. At that time most of the circuses and the menageries were separate attractions and developed in competition to each other (Coup 1901, Hoh and Rough 1990).

On 14 January 1835, a group of 135 farmers and menagerie men involved in the circus business gathered in the ballroom of The Elephant Hotel in Somers, New York, and signed the *Articles of Association of the Zoological Institute* which formalized the menagerie business. It was mainly a merger of the eight main menagerie organizations: June, Titus, Angevine & Company; Raymond & Ogden; Lewis Bailey & Co.; Purdy, Welch & Macomber; J. R. And W. Howe, Jr. & Co.; Kelley, Raymond & Co.; Mead, Miller & Co.; Kelley, Berry & Waring; and, Ganung & Strang & Co. All of the men whether menagerie owners and managers, or individuals, whose business relied on their shows, signed the articles of incorporation controlling thirteen menageries and three affiliated circuses. The document set routes and performance schedules, monopolizing the animal show business in the East. *The Zoological Institute* absorbed the sixteen menageries in the country, whose combined worth in animals and equipment was $300,000. It has been suggested that this document was the "birth certificate" of the American circus. The economic panic of 1837 closed the Institute. The name *Zoological Institute* was used for a number of years after by the exhibiting companies. After 1837, John J. June, Lewis B. Titus, and Caleb S. Angevine (all from North Salem), along with Jesse Smith and Gerard and Thaddeus Crane, formed something that they called "The Syndicate" with which they maintained a firm monopoly on the menagerie and circus businesses until 1877. They became known as *The Flatfoots* because they put their foot down against any competitor moving into their eastern territory (Somers Historical Society ND., Westchester County N.D., Virtual Archives N.D., Hoh and Rough 1990, Chindahl 1959, Johnson 1990).

In April of 1836, P.T. Barnum joined Aaron Turner's traveling circus company as ticket-seller, secretary and treasurer, at thirty dollars a month and one-fifth of the entire profits. The circus started from Danbury traveling to West Springfield, Massachusetts, on April 26. Aaron Turner, was a self-made man, who had acquired a large fortune by his industry. He believed that any man with health and common sense could become rich if he only resolved to be so, and he was very proud of the fact that he began the world with no advantages, no education, and without a shilling. In December 1836 Turner disbanded his circus. Barnum bought four of his horses and two wagons and headed out as *Barnum's Grande Scientific and Musical Theatre.* On May 1837, some state 1838, Barnum disbanded his circus and returned home (Culhane 1991, Kunhardt et al 1995).

The Panic of 1837 dropped the price of New York real estate by 50%. The economic crash led to a three-year depression which opened the opportunity for the middle class to open penny newspapers, publishing houses, theaters, and museums (Kunhardt et al 1995).

In 1837, Hackaliah Bailey of Westport, New York, brought 526 acres of land surrounding the intersection of the Leesburg and Columbia Turnpikes naming the purchase *Bailey's Crossroads.* It became the circus winter headquarters with a barn to house the animals. A tent was utilized for shows before the troupe went on tour in warmer weather. In the same year "General" Rufus Welch brought from Capetown, South Africa, an Egyptian giraffe, which he called the cameoleopard (SHOUA n.d., Vail 1933). *Raymond &*

Waring's Circus & Menagerie were also touring that year (Bogdan 1988).

Wittman (2012) wrote:

> In just two generations the population of the United States more than tripled. It exploded from five million at the turn of the century to over seventeen million in 1840, pushing westward through the Ohio River Valley and beyond the Mississippi. These new markets in cities, towns, and provincial backwaters welcomed the kind of traveling entertainment that the new mobile circus business offered. The decades bracketed by the Panic of 1819 and the Panic of 1837 were also economically prosperous, encouraging a wave of entrepreneurs to try to make their fortune with a touring show.

Moses Kimball purchased the *New England Museum* in1838, and then relocated to Lowell, Maine, to found the *Lowell Museum*, 1840. A year later he opened the *Boston Museum* (Wiki 2019).

In 1840, 30-35 circuses came into existence within a 25-mile circle around Brewster, New York. There were almost traffic jams due to the number of touring circuses in the North Atlantic seaboard, but few toured the middle west (Jensen 1975).

After 1840 the usage of circus tents became the norm. They allowed a rapid set-up and take-down for any area where the circus stopped and wished to attract customers. (Hoh and Rough 1990).

In 1840 Jeremiah "Jeey" Mabie, Edmund F. Mabie, and Seth Howes organized a circus, the *Mabie Circus*, with its first performance in Patterson, New York.

Dan Rice, born 23 January 1823, was most famously known as a clown. In 1841, he was presenting a pig, "Sybil," who could do many tricks, including the ability to tell time. He was a clown in various circuses as well as an animal trainer, songwriter, commentator, political humorist, strong man, actor, director, producer, dancer, and politician. He coined a number of expressions, including: "jump on the band wagon," while campaigning for Zachary Taylor as president, suggesting that Taylor campaign on the circus bandwagon. At one time he had a one horse show which competitors mocked him saying that he was a "one horse show." He utilized that expression as meaning the putting on of a good show. "Hey, Rube!" came into the circus lexicon in 1848 in New Orleans when a troupe member was attacked by a mob and he yelled to his friend Reuben, "Hey, Rube!" This was changed to mean "come help in this fight." He combined in his shows animals, acrobats, and clowns. As a star of the one-ring circus, he achieved national prominence as an equestrian jester. In 1844 he joined *Spalding's North American Circus*. In 1848 the circus was renamed the *Dan Rice's Circus*. In New Orleans in 1852, he managed *Dan Rice's Great Hippodrome and Menagerie* (Carlyon 2001).

By 1841 New York City was the third largest city in the world with about 300,000 population (Kunhardt et al 1995).

In this same year, Edmund F. Mabie, Jeremiah "Jeey" Mabie, and Nathan A and Seth Howes organized and presented to the public the now named *New York Circus*, sometimes advertised as *The Olympic Circus* (Slout 2010). Chindahl (1959) gave the date as 1840 citing documents from 1867 and 1882. Their winter quarters were in Brewster, New York (Jensen 1975).

As early as 1806, in England on the Liverpool Stage there was a troupe performing under the name of *The Olympic Circus* (Broadbent 1908). Whether the organizers of the American circus were aware of that event is problematic. The English circus had such events as equestrian, tight rope performances, riders, gymnasts, and clowns.

The New York State Agricultural Society was founded by a collection of farmers, legislators, and others interested in promoting various aspects of agriculture. They established in 1841, in Syracuse, New York, *The New York State Fair*, which included speeches, animal exhibits, plowing contests, and samples of farm and family goods. At the fair in 1848, or 1849, a 50-foot tall, iron and oaken wheel with wooden bucket cars (4 adults or 6 children) was constructed by two Erie Canal workers, Samuel Hurst and James Hulholland. The wheel was counterbalanced and manually operated by a system of ropes. It was sold to a hotel owner who put it on Baldwin Island and later at the Albany, New York fair (Schramm 1839, Anderson 1992).

As a small side comment (O'Callaghan 1868), New Amsterdam (eventually New York City) passed on 30 September 1641:

ORDINANCE Of the Director and Council of New Netherland, establishing an annual Fair at New Amsterdam.

> Be it known hereby to all persons, that the Director and Council of New Netherland have ordained that henceforth there shall be held annually at Fort Amsterdam a Cattle Fair on the 15th of October, and a fair for Hogs on the 1st of November. Whosoever hath any thing to sell or to buy can regulate himself accordingly.

Done 30th September and affixed at said Fort.

It does not seem that this concept of "Fair" continued into the future but the Syracuse State Fair idea does now occur across the nation as state and county fairs.

The *Tammany Museum* established in 1790, moved in 1830 to a larger five-story marble building which eventually became *Scuder's American Museum* (Kunhardt et al 1995).

In 1842 Phineas Taylor Barnum bought the museum from John Scudder and added new exhibits along with zoo-like exhibits and a freak show. Huge panels on the outside of the building depicted exotic animals. Beyond the exhibition halls, there was a funhouse and performing animals and live animals on display, including giraffes, and whales in a gigantic tank. Visitors could watch performances by glass blowers, magicians, fortune tellers, and phrenologists. There was also an oyster saloon, rooftop garden, and museum shop. It was the first combination of gaudy display and entertainment, including the instruction of and performance of dramas including Shakespeare. He and his family lived in a ground floor apartment that had been the billiard hall.

Barnum (1855) wrote:

> As outside clerk for the Bowery Amphitheatre Barnum learned that the collection of curiosities comprising Scudder's American Museum, at the corner of Broadway and Ann Street, was for sale. [The building was a five-story, corner building] It belonged to the daughters of Mr. Scudder, and was conducted for their benefit by John Furzman, under the authority of Mr. John Heath, administrator. The price asked for the entire collection was fifteen thousand dollars. It had cost its

founder, Mr. Scudder, probably fifty thousand dollars, and from the profits of the establishment he had been able to leave a large competency to his children. The Museum, however, had been for several years a losing concern, and the heirs were anxious to sell it. Looking at this property, I thought I saw that energy, tact and liberality, were only needed to make it a paying institution, and I determined to purchase it if possible. The Museum building belonged to Mr. Francis W. Olmsted, a retired merchant.

Barnum (1872) also wrote:

In 1865, the space occupied for my Museum purposes was more than double what it was in 1842. The Lecture Room, originally narrow, ill-contrived and inconvenient, was so enlarged and improved that it became one of the most commodious and beautiful amusement halls in the City of New York. At first, my attractions and inducements were merely the collection of curiosities by day, and an evening entertainment, consisting of such variety performances as were current in ordinary shows. Then Saturday afternoons, and, soon afterwards, Wednesday afternoons were devoted to entertainments and the popularity of the Museum grew so rapidly that I presently found it expedient and profitable to open the great Lecture Room every afternoon, as well as every evening, on every week-day in the year. The first experiments in this direction, more than justified my expectations, for the day exhibitions were always more thronged than those of the evening. Of course I made the most of the holidays, advertising extensively and presenting extra inducements; nor did attractions elsewhere seem to keep the crowd from coming to the Museum. On great holidays, I gave as many as twelve performances to as many different audiences.

By degrees the character of the stage performances was changed. The transient attractions of the Museum were constantly diversified, and educated dogs, industrious fleas, automatons, jugglers, ventriloquists, living statuary, tableaux, gipsies, Albinoes, fat boys, giants, dwarfs, rope-dancers, live "Yankees," pantomime, instrumental music, singing and dancing in great variety, dioramas, panoramas, models of Niagara, Dublin, Paris, and Jerusalem; Hannington's dioramas of the Creation, the Deluge, Fairy Grotto, Storm at Sea; the first English Punch and Judy in this country, Italian Fantoccini, mechanical figures, fancy glass-blowing, knitting machines and other triumphs in the mechanical arts; dissolving views, American Indians, who enacted their warlike and religious ceremonies on the stage,—these, among others, were all exceedingly successful.

The concept of museums was a new idea which slowly grew. Before they became state-supported institutions they were commercial or "proprietary" museums (Wall 2013). Many were for entertainment, education, and spectacle. These museums were often called "dime museums," and were an entertainment that was popular in Europe as early as the 16th century (Kelly n.d.2).

Samuel Barret Edes, an American sea captain in 1822 bought a "mermaid," constructed from a juvenile monkey's head and torso sewn to the back half of a fish, from some

Japanese sailors for $6,000. He displayed it in London. In 1842 his son sold it to Moses Kimall (Bondeson 1999, Wiki 2020b).

Moses Kimball came from New York City in the spring of 1842 to visit Barnum and leased him The Fejee Mermaid (so named by Barnum), for $12.50 a week. A poster from the *Boston Museum*, Vermont, dated 15 September 1850, in the *Barre Patriot*, of Barre, Maine, advertising the Fejee Mermaid, stated (Wiki 2019) that the:

> FEJEE MERMAID which was exhibited in most of the principal cities of America, in the years 1840, '41, and '42, to the wonder and astonishment of thousands of naturalists and other scientific persons, whose previous doubts of the existence of such an astonishing creature were entirely removed . . .

Which suggests that Kimball was as full of humbug as Barnum.

Barnum bought (with Kimball) Ruben Peale's *New York Museum* in 1842, and by himself, the *Baltimore Museum* in 1845, and then *New York's Chinese Collection*, and *Peale's Philadelphia Museum* (ASHP 2002, Johnson 1990, Kunhardt et al 1995)).

Audiences were curious about the world. Barnum advertised his museum as an "encyclopedic synopsis of everything worth seeing in this curious world." It became the single greatest attraction in America. In the years 1842-1865, approximately 38 million visitors passed through the museum's doors (Wall 2013) among them Henry and William James, Charles Dickens, and Edward VII, then prince of Wales (Wallace n.d.) The population in the United States in 1840 was 12,866,00 rising to 31,443,321 in 1860. Barnum started tours as *P.T. Barnum's Grand Traveling American Museum.*

Barnum saw himself for most of his life as part of "the show business." He was the first person to use that terminology (Kunhardt et al 1995).

John Robinson formed his circus, The *John Robinson Circus,* which toured 1842-1911 under the ownership of four generations: John Robinson I (1807-1888), John Robinson II (1843-1921), John Robinson III (1872-1935), and John Robinson IV (1893-1954) (anon n.d.)

In 1842 the *June, Titus and Angevine's Menagerie* advertised that the only living giraffe on the American continent was in their show. The *Welch & Mann's Circus* included contortionists and acrobats (Vail 1933, Chindahl 1959).

In 1843, Nathan Howes left *The Mabie Circus* and Seth B. Howes took over management. In 1846 Howes sold his interest and the circus was renamed *The Grande Olympic Arena and United States Circus.* This was the first time a circus traveled into the western states (Slout 2010). None of the small traveling circuses before 1847 went further west than Buffalo (Greenwood 2015).

Seth Howes retired in 1870 worth $70 million dollars, about $1 billion dollars in today's money (Wall 2013).

In 1847 the Mabie owned circus, the *Grande Olympic Arena and United States Circus,* after six years of touring paused in Delavan, Territory of Wisconsin, on 28 August, at a watering stop at the great lake just outside of the town (Chindahl 1959, Jensen1975).

The town, created in 1836, by Harry and Samuel Phoenix, was named by them after Edwin Cornelius Delavan, a wealthy businessman famed for his anti-booze stance in New York. The settlers were mostly Puritans (Jensen 1975). A town in Illinois was formed in 1837 by settlers from New England who named it Delavan.

The Mabie brothers, looking for land to establish a new home base, bought 400 acres with two barns for $3,700 from Nicholas Thorne, a local farmer. The Mabies built a new house and barns for their winter settlement. Their holdings eventually expanded to 1,000 acres. The circus bought many of its supplies from the local businesses. In 1848 Edmund Mabie, with a cash bonus, convinced state crew to run the plank road through the village as the road headed for Racine. Edmund offered, $2,500, seven years later, to the Mississippi-Racine Railroad to include Delavan on its route (Hoh and Rough 1990, Jensen 1975, Lahey 2019). In 1963 the town erected a monument that listed on their circus history, "Delavan's Circus Colony."

In 1845 the Mabie's bought two elephants, Romeo and his mate Juliet, from *P.T. Barnum's Asiatic Caravan, Menagerie and Museum* which was going out of business. Romeo was one of the largest Indian elephants exhibited in the United States. The Mabie's made much about Romeo's being "The Killer Elephant" (Jensen 1975).

Adam Forepaugh made his first fortune during the Civil War selling horses to the U.S. government.

It had been suggested that the Mabies adopted in 1857 the circus dining tent rather than patronize local innkeepers (Chindahl 1959).

James Anthony McGinnis, born 4 July 1847, renamed himself James Anthony Bailey. He was orphaned when he was eight years old. When he was a teenager he was hired by Frederic Harrison, a nephew of Hachaliah Bailey. Frederic gave hin a job as his assistant in his circus. McGinnis eventually changed his name using the Bailey surname.

From 1847 to 1894, performers from more than 26 different circuses called Delavan home with the place becoming known as the *19th Century Circus Capital* (Lahey 2019).

Late in the circus season, in the fall of 1848, the *Welch, Delevan & Nathan's Circus* exhibited "the 80 somerset man," at the Alhambra Theatre in New York City. He would do 80 somersets in a row. "Somerset" is what we, today, call somersault, which is defined as "an acrobatic movement in which a person turns head over heels in the air or on the ground and lands or finishes on their feet" (Chindahl 1959).

By 1849, the Mabie circus had 670 horses and 8 wagons, the tent was an 85 foot round top. By the 1880's the *Grande Olympic Arena and United States Circus* had the largest canvas of any circus (Jensen 1975).

Joseph A. Rowe's *Olympic Circus* brought his troupe overland from Maraicabo, Venezuela, to the Pacific shore at Guayaquil, Ecuador, in November 1848. He had been traveling with his circus through Cuba and Central America since 1846 (Wittman 2012). Then they traveled from Panama on the 286 ton bark *Tasso* with a crew of 21, and arrived in San Francisco on 12 October 1849. Barks have three masts, with the foremast and mainmast square rigged and the mizzenmast fore-and-aft rigged (Solem 1997). They opened on Kearney Street to be remembered thereafter as California's "pioneer" circus. He exhibited as *Rowe's Olympic Circus* with equestrian displays, a clown and rider, rope-dancers and acrobats under a tent (Chindahl 1959, Wittman 2012). Admission to the box seats was $5.00 while back east the price was 50¢ (Hoh and Rough 1990, St. Leon 2014). In 1850 he took his circus on a tour of the Pacific Islands and Australia. In

1857, Rowe returned to California and toured the mining districts of the interior of the state as the *Rowe and Co., Pioneer Circus of California* (Chindahl 1959, Culhane 1991).

The form of the circus become a traveling tent-show, with a menagerie, run by business men while the European model was based on and controlled by the performing families.

George Fox Bailey, Hachaiah's, nephew, bought in 1851, six cages of animals, from the Zoological Institute, and combined them with several elephants in his show (Johnson 1990).

William Hoyt of Dupont, Indiana, published a description of how to produce music through a device operated by steam in the *Dayton (Ohio) Journal and Advertiser*, 1 April 1851. It was essentially the same as a music box with a rotating drum with pins that opened or closed steam whistles of one or more octaves. J.C. Stoddard of Worcester, Massachusetts, patented (No. 13,668), on 9 October 1855, a *New Musical Instrument to be Played by the Agency of Steam or Highly Compressed Air*. This became known as the steam calliope utilizing a keyboard rather than a fixed drum of pins. His original intention was to call people to worship, responding to the evangelical fervor characteristic of the New England populace during the 19th Century. It was also used on an excursion on the Boston & Maine Railroad, Worcester to Fitchburg, for a Fremont political meeting in 1856 (Chindahl 1959, Lajoie 2017, Vail 1933).

The term bandwagon (or band wagon) first appeared in P. T. Barnum's autobiography (Barnum 1855). Latter folk called the ornate wagons "tableau wagons" due to the ornate carvings mounted on their sides and the paint and gilding that enhanced the carvings (Kathleen 2019).

Nixon & Kemp's *Great Eastern Show*, in 1857 had two units to operate the calliope, one steam traction engine, and the other having the whistles, keyboards, and musician's seat, with steam being supplied by the first unit. Spalding and Rogers added one to the steamboat *James Raymond* the same year. Sands, Nathan & Co. of the *American and English Circus*, utilized a single unit while Levi J. North's *National Circus* advertised *The Calliope, producing music by steam, to be heard ten miles off.* In 1859 Sands, Nathan & Co. added another calliope (Chindahl 1959).

Barnum, Seth B. Howes, and Lewis Lent toured, from1851-1853, *Barnum's Great Asiatic Caravan, Museum and Menagerie* under tent. William Cameron Coup (born in 1837 in Mount Pleasant, Indiana), aged 14, or 15, or 16(?), worked for the circus as a roustabout, a circus worker who erects and dismantles tents, cares for the grounds, and handles animals and equipment.(Slout 2000, Chindahl 1959).

Dr. Gilbert R. Spalding had been the owner of a paint and drug store from1840-1845. From his drug store endeavor he had acquired the title of "Doctor." He became the owner of the circus of Sam H. Nicols around 1843 due to the debt that Nicols had run up for paint and cash loans. Spaulding renamed the circus *Spalding's North American Circus* and ended his paint and drug store business (Slout 1997, Chindal 1959).

Hiram Older had traded in a saw mill located in Janesville, Wisconsin, for $5,000, which he used to buy a third interest in the Mabie circus in 1849 (Slout 2010).

Charles Rogers, an English equestrian, the son of an English performer, John Rogers, came to the United States in 1816 with James West's circus. He joined Spalding's circus as the principal rider and bought into the circus in 1848. This circus is credited with using "quarter poles" to support the canvas between the center pole and the side poles (Slout 2010, Chindahl 1959).

Shortly thereafter Spalding and Rogers launched in Cincinnati in1851, the 200-foot *Floating Circus Palace* which was reported as costing $42,000 (over a million dollars today), It was an elaborate two-story barge, with a four-foot draft, that contained a regulation circus ring and a stage. It was twice the size of New Orleans' St. James Theater, the city's largest building in 1851, and had 3,400 seats on two decks. In addition to the 42-foot circus ring area, it also had a museum with "100,000 curiosities of past years." It was towed by the steamboat *James Raymond* built by the Cincinnati company in 1853. It had a stage for minstrel shows, staterooms for the performers, crew quarters, a galley, mess hall, and laundry. In 1854 they leased the *Van Amburgh & Raymond Menagerie* and exhibited it in the *Floating Circus Palace.* In 1855 they added the steamboat *Banjo* to their fleet. The *Banjo* was the first of its kind on the river with seating for an audience (Merrick 1909). The *Floating Circus Palace* visited ports up and down the Mississippi and Ohio Rivers, doing this until the Civil War broke out (Hoh and Rough 1990). The *Floating Circus Palace* burned early in the spring of 1865. Plate III in Chindahl states it happened in New Albany, Indiana {but a wide search failed to find anything about the vessel burning} (Chindahl 1959, Hémard 2009, Slout 1997).

The Mabies circus had grown so large that they split it into two touring units in 1852, one the *Mabie Bros. Grande Olympic Arena and United States Circus* and the other *P.A. Older's Great United State Circus* (Jensen 1975).

Spaulding and Rogers were among the first to experiment with railroad travel in 1853 exhibiting in Detroit the *Railroad Circus and Crystal Palace*. Greenwood (2015) said that they claimed that they had done this in 1856.

Coup joined the Mabies *Grande Olympian Arena and U.S. Circus* in 1853, working as the sideshow manager with Harry Buckley. Eventually Coup secured the sideshow privileges of the *E. F. & J Mabie Circus* until 1866. He did the same thing with the Yankee Robinson Circus until 1869 as well as being an Assistant Manager and sideshowman of the *Yankee Circus* (Coup 1901, Slout 2000).

The First Congregation Church in Delavan replaced their building with a new one in 1855. The Mabie's bought the old church, relocated it to their lands, and converted the building into menagerie winter housing. They had a lion, lioness, two three-year-old lions, a leopard, a cheetah, a South American jaguar, a black tiger, a hyena, a bear, a ciret cat, a mountain cat, a cougar, a panther, a kangaroo, a badger, a white racoon, a pelican, an emu, rare birds, monkeys, and other animals housed inside the building. They were placed in cages around the walls with a large iron stove providing heat over the winter (Jensen 1975).

H. Buckley & Co.'s National Circus, was organized in Delavan, Wisconsin, in 1857, by Harry Buckley, manager. In 1858, the *Buckley-Babcock North American Circus* was on the road for two years concluding in the Caribbean aboard a sailing vessel.

In 1858 Spaulding and Rogers ran an advertisement in Davenport on 26 May (Chindahl 1959). The following quote gives some idea as to what kinds of attractions they felt the audience would enjoy:

> Mons. Eugene Goddard will make one Grande
> Balloon Ascension with his newly invented

Parachute Attachment and his newly
discovered Process of Inflation at 5 o'clock
(process of inflation commencing at 4 P.M.)
Under the management of Messers. Spaulding
and Rogers who have devoted their steamers
James Raymond and Banjo exclusively to the
enterprise. Admission is 25 cents. The balloon
tickets admit spectators inside the Tent to
witness the process of inflation (an interesting
and thrilling operation).

Obviously, humbug was not restricted to P.T. Barnum.

In 1860, Frank Howes imported the first hippopotamus. It was bought from Gerald C. Quick and Joseph Cushing's circus touring England from the United States (Slout 2010, Williams 2017).

The elephant soon to be named "Jumbo" was born around 1860 and was captured when his mother was killed by hunters. He was sold by Sudanese elephant hunters to eventually wind up in the London Zoological Society. By 1882 he was 12 feet tall at the shoulders [other citations suggested 10 feet, *Wikipedia - Jumbo*] and weighed around six and a half tons (Culhane 1991, Kunhardt et al 1991).

Coup described what a wagon show traveling in the southwest saw when traveling on the roads (Culhane 1991):

over such wretched constructed highways that
the slightest fall of rain was sufficient to
convert them into rivers of mud. The heavy
wagons would sink to their hubs in the mire
and the whole train would be stopped.

P.T. Barnum bought in 1862, the *Boston Aquarial and Zoological Gardens* and renamed them the *Barnum Boston*

Aquarial Gardens. He remodeled the space and opened the collections to the public in June 1862. That summer he wandered around the Caribbean collecting tropical fish and one sea lion. The gardens became a show-hall with Madame Lanista wrestling with snakes, a dog show, a baby show, plus dramatic performances (including Tom Thumb, Colonel Nugget and the Albino Family) running from December 1862 to 14 February 1863. The contents of the Gardens were moved in 1863 to the *American Museum* in New York (Wikivisually n.d.3, New England Aquarium 2011)

In 1863, George Fox Bailey, the son of Hachaliah Bailey, became a the manager for the *Turner Circus.* He had married the Turner daughter, and later inherited the circus and renamed it *The George F. Bailey Great American Show.* It performed nationwide from 1863 to 1871.

In 1863 Dan Castello started *Castello and Van Vleck's Mammoth Show* with a new tent that seated 2,000. Matt Van Vleck, had been the postmaster and the owner of a lead mine in Fairplay, Wisconsin (Slout 2000). John H. Glenroy joined the circus. He was known as the first to make a backward somersault riding bareback on a horse (Wilson 2012). Within a few months, Van Vleck accepted George W. DeHaven as an associate member of the circus.

In 1864 *Howes & Norton's Champion Circus* was created in Chicago

Costello formed a new circus in 1864 and traveled on the 145-ton stern-wheeler steamboat *Jeanette Roberts* up and down the Mississippi and Ohio Rivers. (Slout 2009, Peterson 1970).

Barnum made arrangements in 1865 with the *Van Amburgh Menagerie Company* to unite the collection of living animals with his new museum. He called his new company

the *Barnum and Van Amburgh Museum and Menagerie Company.*
Barnum owned forty percent, the *Van Amburgh Company* held
sixty percent. The menagerie traveled in the summer and
wintered in the museum (Barnum 1888).

Castello formed a venture with William Cameron
Coup in 1869, *Dan Costello's Great Circus and Egyptian Caravan.*
It traveled by boat on the 146-foot, propeller driven, *Benton,*
throughout the Great Lakes (Michigan, Superior, Huron),
visiting port cities large and small. The circus toured the
Upper Midwest, both overland and by boat and featured
eight camels, bought for $80 per head, originally utilized by
the U.S. Army Camel Corps.

The Camel Corps was the brainchild of U.S. Army LT
George H. Crosman in 1836 who felt that it would aid the
westward expansion into the inhospitable terrain and climate
faced by the pioneers and the settlers. On 3 March 1855,
Congress agreed and passed the Shield amendment to the
appropriation bill, resolving:

> And be it further enacted, that the sum of
> $30,000 be, and the same is hereby
> appropriated under the direction of the War
> Department in the purchase and importation
> of camels and dromedaries to be employed for
> military purposes.

The ship *Supply* delivered on 14 May 1856, thirty-four
camels, which included Bactrian (two-humped), dromedaries
(one-humped), nineteen Arabian, one Tunis burden, one
Arabian calf, and one Tuili or booghdee camel, to Indianola,
Texas.

In 1864, Adam John Forepaugh, independently
wealthy, sold 44 horses to John V. "Pogey" O'Brien for $9,000

so he could start the *Tom King Excelsior Circus*. O'Brien could not repay the loan so Forepaugh assumed partial ownership of the circus. He and O'Brien in 1865 purchased the *Jerry Mabie Menagerie* and created two circuses with their combined assets: The *Great National Circus* and the *Dan Rice Circus*. Forepaugh sold the *Great National Circus* and put the *Dan Rice Circus* under his own name. Tom King was the featured performer, considered as the greatest of the leapers. Forepaugh had once worked as both a horse trainer and animal dealer in Pennsylvania, Ohio, and New York. During the Civil War he had sold horses to both the North and the South (Slout 1997, Jensen 1975, Chindahl 1959).

Circus leapers would run down a very long ramp (runway) and bound onto a hickory springboard. This would catapult them 75-100 feet through the air. They would often execute somersaults or twists in mid-air (Jensen 1975).

The advent of the Civil War effectively halted the camel experiment.

On 26 February 1864, the thirty-seven camels were sold for $1,945, or $52.56 per camel. On 6 March 1866, forty-four camels were put on the auction block, bringing $1,364, or $31 per camel (Hawkins 2014).

Three sisters living in Baraboo, Wisconsin, through marriage, developed an extended circus family. Marie Juliar married August Ringling (family name changed from Rungeling) and gave birth to the seven Ringling Brothers and one Ringling sister. Mary Juliar married Gottlieb Gollmar. Their five sons formed Gollmar Brothers Circus in 1891. Katherine Juliar's husband Henry Moeller and their two sons ran a wagon and carriage shop that provided wagons for the family's two circuses (Reid 2010).

The circus visited McGregor, Iowa, located next to the

Mississippi River with the steamboat *Will S. Hayes* pulling a barge loaded with the circus wagons (North and Hatch 1960). The steamboat was about 200 feet long and 18 feet wide, containing 45 large rooms. There were 108 electric lights on board with one 8,000 candle power electric light facing forward and one focusing for general use about the deck and for use in landing (Ellwanger 1919).

Five of the Ringling Brothers went down to watch the circus unload. They attended the circus with a free pass as their uncle had done some leather work for the circus and had been given a free pass. This stimulated the brothers to begin their careers as entertainers and eventually circus owners (Culhane 1991).

Forepaugh separated the menagerie from the big ring. He apparently felt that this would attract church goers who might be leery of the "sinful" attractions of circus acts while still enjoying seeing the "exotic" menagerie animals (Slout 1997, Jensen 1975, Chindahl 1959).

In July, 1865, Barnum's Museum building burned down along with 18 adjacent buildings. He reopened a new museum in a three-story granite building, September 1868 (Kunhardt et al 1995).

In 1866, the *American Society for the Prevention of Cruelty to Animals* was formed. The ASPCA director Henry Bergh objected to Barnum about the public feeding of live rabbits to snakes (ASHP 2002).

Barnum replied (ASHP 2002):

New York, March 4th, 1867

Henry Bergh, Esq.

Dear Sir:

On my return from the West in December last, I found your letter of December 11th, addressed to this association, threatening us with punishment if we permitted our Boa Constrictors to eat their food alive. You furthermore declared, that our assertion that these reptiles would die, unless permitted to eat their food alive, was "false in theory and practice, for no living creature will allow itself to perish with hunger, with food before it, be the ailment dead or alive." I enclose a letter from Professor Agassiz, denying your statement.

Jean Louis Rodolphe Agassiz, a Swiss-American biologist and geologist was widely recognized as an innovative and prodigious scholar of Earth's natural history. He received doctor of philosophy and medical degrees at both Erlangen and Munich. He emigrated to the United States in 1847 after visiting Harvard University and had become professor of zoology and geology at Harvard, heading its Lawrence Scientific School, and founded the *Museum of Comparative Zoology* (Lurie 1988).

Barnum's *Barnum & Van Amburgh's Museum and Menagerie* toured in 1867 during the summer months and then went inside the museum during the winter months (Slout 2000).

Barnum's new museum burned to the ground in March of 1868, during a bitter winter. After this Barnum retired (Kunhardt et al 1995).

By 1868 there were 42,229 miles of railroads in operation with the golden spike connecting the east coast and the west coast (Chindahl 1959).

The Castello circus traveled west by train after the 1869

completion of the transcontinental railroad (Jensen 1975). It was the first circus to go coast to coast (Slout 2000).

1869 is considered as the most economically disastrous for the circus business since the beginning. It was estimated that out of the twenty or more of the most well known circuses only about six ended financially stable by the end of the year.

By 1870 south-central Ohio became the center of the United States population. This was due to the western migration of settlers after the Civil War. (Slout 2000).

In 1870 Barnum met with Costello, the owner of his own circus, and William C. Coup, his manager, and agreed to create a new circus, planned for 1871.

The quote "There's a sucker born every minute, but none of them ever die" is often attributed to P. T. Barnum. The source of the quote is most likely the famous con-man Joseph ("Paper Collar" Joe) Bessimer. Forepaugh attributed the quote to Barnum in a newspaper interview in an attempt to discredit him. However, Barnum never denied making the quote. It is said that he thanked Forepaugh for the free publicity he had given him.

Barnum was famous for talking about humbug as something that the public enjoyed.

Many people are familiar with the term, "Bah, Humbug" uttered by Scrooge in Dicken's story. But, in Dicken's time the term meant "nonsense." By Barnum's time the term meant:

A befooling trick (Partridge 1961);
A sham, imposter or imposture (Beale 1989);
A hoax or deception, a person who practices to deceive (Rawson 1989).

Many of Barnum's presentations were humbug which he felt was a form of entertainment.

Gregg Mangan (2019) wrote:

> While there is no record of Barnum ever saying, "There is a sucker born every minute," biographer Wallace wrote that the showman did say "the American people liked to be humbugged." If "humbugging" and exaggeration pleased his audiences, Barnum saw no harm in it.

Mansky (2017) wrote:

> As it was "generally understood," Barnum wrote in the book, the term humbug "consists in putting on glittering appearances—outside show—novel expedients, by which to suddenly arrest public attention, and attract the public eye and ear." And Barnum wanted to make it clear such a practice was justified. "[T]here are various trades and occupations which need only notoriety to insure success," he claimed, concluding no harm, no foul, so long as at the end of the day customers felt like they got their money's worth.

Cook (2001) wrote, in looking at "deception' from an historical perspective:

> In the nineteenth-century arts of deception, then, illusionism and realism were always interconnected – at least as aesthetic antipodes. That was the discovery that first made Barnum famous. There was no need to choose between illusion and realism. The public was amused even when it was conscious of being deceived.

Kunhardt (et al 1995) quoted Barnum as saying that the term "humbug" rather than"notoriety" meant:"

> "Putting on glittering appearance by which to suddenly arrest public attention and attract the public eye and ear."

Barnum further suggested:

> When customers are once attracted they never fail to get their money's worth.

> If the public was not well served by a showman, then he deserved to fail.

> "I don't believe in 'duping the public', but I believe in first attracting and pleasing them."

> "The greatest humbug of all is the man who believes . . . that everything and everybody are humbugs."

As a small side discussion we can say that today we often speak of *the suspension of reality*, which means the suspension of disbelief, or, willing suspension of disbelief, that is, that the individual has decided to ignore reality when engaged in some activity. Sagan (1997) suggested that it was "a willing suspension of skepticism, or the willing suspension of disbelief." This could be people who: still read comics or illustrated novels about superheroes; watch movies about monsters; characters human and non-human, of all varieties; read books treating the same topics; join or create fan clubs to discuss the ways and wherefores of those characters; engage in computer or televison games or series that run for years; theatrical plays; various forms of political and religious arguments; stage magicians; and so forth and so on. While P.T. Barnum's career is interesting/fascinating and the subject of much speculation, the things listed in this paragraph are merely today's version of "humbug," now simply called "entertainment," an equally active money-making activity.

Once Costello and Coup had Barnum on board, Coup began to collect various ingredients for the new circus: large quantities of canvas, all manner of wagons; the finest horses from the bluegrass country of Kentucky. By 20 March 1871, everything was loaded on ten railroad cars including the trained animals and circus paraphernalia, in Delavan, and headed for New York to collect more performers and workmen: 75 full-time employees, as well as 60 stars and secondary performers. The circus Big Top seated 5,000 and all the tents covered three acres (Jensen 1975, Culhane 1991, Kunhardt et al 1995).

Barnum wanted a complete amusement organization: circus; museum (the first time such a thing was connected with a circus); and, menagerie. It was all separated in three large exhibition tents with an additional 5-8 horse tents for thirty head and a dining tent with a wagon cookhouse, ten tents in all. It was called *P. T. Barnum's Grand Traveling Museum, Menagerie and Circus.* S.H. Hurd, Barnum's son-in-law, was made treasurer. The tour was confined to the northeastern states: New Jersey, Connecticut, Massachusetts, Rhode Island, New Hampshire, Maine, Vermont, and New York (Chindahl 1959, Slout 2000, Kunhardt et al 1995).

The museum, 1,000 feet long, had an array of mechanical figures along with a number of objects of "curiosity;" wax figures, artillery pieces, bone fragments, etc.

The menagerie, in Barnum's view, was second in importance: 12 camels, 4 lions, 1 rhinoceros, 2 elephants, with zebras, gnus, yaks, elands, tawny and black leopards, kangaroos, white deer, boars, various birds and monkeys, and eventually water tanks with sea lions from Alaska (Slout 2000).

Barnum started, in 1871, a 24-page illustrated newspaper, *P.T. Barnum's Advance Courier*, with 50,000 free copies distributed in every town a week before the circus arrived (Kunhardt et al 1995).

Through the 1870s and into the 1880s, Forepaugh and Barnum had the two largest circuses in the nation. Forepaugh had more animals and tended to pay higher salaries to his much-favored European talent.

On 28 April 1872 Coup had decided to keep the show on the rails, now 66,171 miles of railroad. They utilized gangplanks between the flat cars for leading horses, elephants, and other stock in and out of the stock cars. Uniformly-sized flat cars were built so the draft horses could tug the heavy wagons up the ramp end of the train and then forward over steel plates bridging the gaps between the flatcars. They had subbing posts to control the descent from flat car ramps to the ground during off-loading of the wagons. There were rented sleepers for performers and musicians, and coaches for the roustabouts. The circus was renamed *P.T. Barnum's Great Traveling Exhibition And World's Fair On Wheels* (Chindahl 1959, Jensen 1975, Culhane 1991). Coup started using specially chartered "excursion trains" to bring people from the nearby small towns to the circus on performance days. These trains had reduced fares and included the ticket price (Slout 2000) An 1872 ad was headed: *The Greatest Show on Earth! Barnum's Magic City*. Across the bottom it read: *P. T. Barnum's Great Traveling World's Fair.*

Seven superior exhibitions in six colossal tents, which, at a challenge of $100,000 is ten times larger than any other show on Earth (Kunhardt et al 1995).

William Washington Cole launched a wagon show in 1872, *W. W. Cole's New York and New Orleans Circus and Menagerie.* In 1873 he began to utilized railroad cars (Chindahl 1959).

Coup began to build what he called the "Greatest Show on Earth" in 1873: repairing/redecorating 150 wagons; having made 24 tents, four held in reserve (with a big top, 300 by 200 feet, seating 13,000 people); refurbishing the rail flat cars; rebuilding passenger cars into sleeping cars winding up with 5 sleeping cars and 6 passenger cars; stock cars for 300 horses; hiring a taxidermist for the 500 birds for the museum cages; ordering enough food for the menagerie, where the animals consumed daily 500 pounds of meat, 500 pounds of hay for the elephants and great quantities for the camels and horses, and100 pounds of saltwater fish for each sea lion. There were 300 workmen. It was first time for the circus to have two rings, one decorated in blue, the other crimson, in the main tent with two groups of performers doing much the same thing. There were 16 changes made in the acts, all but three involved with the two rings. A new steam calliope, 20 feet long, played along the route as the circus train, 62 - 65 cars, approached each city. The circus became known, for awhile, in 1873, as *P.T. Barnum's Great Traveling World's Fair, Consisting of Museum, Menagerie, Caravan, Hippodrome, Gallery of Statuary and Fine Arts, Polytechnic Institute, Zoölogical Garden, and 100,000 Curiosities, Combined with Dan Castello's, Sig Sebastian's, and Mr. D'Atelie's Grande Triple Equestrian and Hippodromatic Exposition* (Hoh and Rough 1990).The total operation was called *P. T. Barnum's Great Traveling World's*

Fair Consisting of Museum, Menagerie, Caravan, Hippodrome, Gallery of Statuary and Fine Arts, Polytechnic Institute (Chindahl 1959, Slout 2000).

At this time Coup was General Manager. Dan Costello Director of Amusements, was in charge of circus performance. S. H. Hurd was treasurer. J. L. Hutchinson was the press agent in sale of Barnum's autobiography. D.S. Thomas was another press agent. James M. Nixon was Superintendent of Amusements, while the Bunnell Brothers operated the sideshow (Slout 2000).

At the end of the season the circus moved into winter quarters in the *American Institute* building in New York City.

James Anthony Bailey bought a half-interest in *Hemmings, Cooper & Whitby Circus* aftershow in 1873 and later became half owner of *Cooper & Bailey's Circus* when he was 29. The depression of 1873 caused the circus of Seth B. Howes to fail. It was bought by Coop & Bailey (Chindahl 1959, Culhane 1991, North and Hatch 1960).

Barnum decided to split the traveling exhibition into two units. Costello sold his interest to Barnum. Coup then decided to do the same thing (Jensen 1975).

Barnum launched a new project *P.T. Barnum's New Rome Hippodrome* in 1874, a place for racing with anything with legs. He acquired the entire block between Fourth and Madison Avenues facing Madison Square. It featured a fifth of a mile oval track for chariot races inside of which was a circus ring (Slout 2000, Cluhane 1991).

In the time period 1873-1883 ten circuses had become railroad shows: W. W. Cole and Height, De Haven & Miles, John Robinson, Forepaugh, Sells Bros., Batcheller & Doris, Burr Robins, Sells Bros' No. 2 Show, Harris Nickel Plate Show, Frank A. Robbins (Chindahl 1959).

In 1874 Barnum hired John V. "Pogey" O'Brien as circus manager. He had previously managed/owned a number of circuses: *Tom King Excelsior Circus, Whitby & Co., Bryan's Circus and Menagerie, Demott & Ward's* and *John O'Brien's World's Fair on Wheels* (Slout 2000).

This time the show moved on wagons. The menagerie and museum were still featured over the ring performance, a two-ring format first utilized by Coup in 1873. The candy, concert, and sideshow became controlled by George H. Batcheller and John B. Doris replacing the Bunnel brothers who transferred their annex to Barnum's Great Roman Hippodrome in New York City (Slout 2000).

Rail travel was utilized by Howes' *Great London Circus* in 1875 and Cooper & Bailey and Adam Forepaugh in 1876. In addition there were ten other circuses traveling about (Slout 2000).

Forepaugh's eighth annual tour in 1874 advertised that they had two rings inside an eighteen-center-pole tent with 60 different species in its menagerie (Slout 2000).

Barnum's hippodrome ended in failure in 1875. It was just too expensive (Slout 2000).

In 1876 the "Flatfoots," Avery Smith, John J. Nathans, George F. Bailey, and Lewis B. June, ran the circus (1876-188) under Barnum's name with a 50-50 arrangement, Barnum receiving 50%, the other people 50%. Barnum had purchased the *Great European Circus and Menagerie* from them and was organizing "the most colossal show ever collected." Barnum was the manager and sole proprietor, Bailey (general superintendent) managed the circus, Nathans (general director) directed performance, June did advance planning and advertising, and Smith (or, perhaps, Thomas P. Jones) was treasurer with S. H. Hurd (financial director). Their tenure ran 1876-1880. The performance in a 150-foot ring with a 50-foot middle piece. Seating was 15 tiers of "blue" seats and 13 tiers of "red" extras. The menagerie was an 80 foot tent with three forty-foot middles, They advertised four circuses: *P. T. Barnum's Hippodrome Heroes; Smith, Nathans & Co.'s Great European Circus; Lowande's Imperial Brazilian Circus,* and, *the Company Carlos.* The museum was supervised by W. L. Jukes while the sideshow, or Annex, was now managed by the Bunnell brothers. They moved on 45 railroad cars (Slout 2000).

The circus traveled through Connecticut, Massachusetts, Rhode Island, New Hampshire, Maine, New Brunswick, Nova Scotia, Vermont, New York State, Pennsylvania, Virginia, and Maryland, ending in New Jersey (Slout 2000).

Barnum and Forepaugh, in 1882, 1884, and 1887, divided the country into exclusive territories to avoid disputes between them.

Equestrian shows dominated the 1878 season with an increase in animals in the menagerie and with the museum loaded with artifacts, people, and mechanical devices (Slout 2000).

In 1878, the Sells Brother now utilized rail with 45 cars with a subsidiary of 44 cars (Culhane 1991).

The 1879 Flatfoot circus had 316 people on salary, 51 railway cars, with 23 baggage wagons, twelve museum cages, five tableau cars, one ticket window, 135 horses, fourteen ponies, and ten elephants. The circus followed the same route as before but added Michigan, Illinois, Missouri, Indiana, Ohio, West Virginia, and Washington, D. C. (Slout 2000).

The 1880 season followed much the same as the

previous year. It was the longest and the most profitable season under the "Flatfoot" management. The 1880s were years of peace and prosperity in the United States. It was also the first year, 1879, that the human cannon-ball act was first performed in the United States by Rosa M. Richter (stage name Zazel), from London, at the Barnum show (Chindahl 1959, Slout 2000, Culhane 1991, Kunhardt et al 1995).

Cooper & Bailey (1879-1880) combined shows: *Howe's Great London Circus, Sanger's Royal British Menagerie, Cooper,* and *Bailey's International Allied Shows.* In 1879 they experimented with electric lights but stopped as being impractical at that time (Chindahl 1959).

At the start of the 1881 circus season Bailey and James H. Hutchinson bought out the Flatfoots and Copper's holding. The consolidated shows were *P. T. Barnum's Greatest Show on Earth, Howe's Great London Circus,* and *Sanger's Royal British Menagerie.* The co-owners were P. T. Barnum, James H. Hutchinson, and James A. Bailey (Chindahl 1959).

Barnum bought the elephant "Jumbo" from the London Zoological Society for $10,000. Barnum utilized the publicists he had in London to get children to write letters protesting the sale. In March 1882, 4,626 people came to say goodbye to the elephant due to this. The attendance to see the elephant the previous day was 214. The Society grossed $50,000 from farewell receptions. In the United States, Jumbo was the greatest circus attraction during the next three and a half years. Jumbo led 30 elephants in a grand parade and after the show gave rides to children, all of which expanded attendance at the circus and spawned a flood of souvenirs of Jumbo. The elephant traveled in what Barnum called "Jumbo's Palace Car," a crimson and gold boxcar with large double doors for easy access to a ramp. Barnum claimed that he had paid $30,000 for the elephant. He earned $3,000 a day for the first three weeks they were back in the United States (Culhane 1991, Elliot 2008, Kunhardt et al 1995).

Five cars and crew to operate a stereopticon were the advance crew in 1882. They preceded each show from 1882 to 1885. Barnum in a lithograph showed the *Exterior View of Our Great City of Tents. The Largest tent ever made. 336,000 yards of canvas* (Chindahl 1959, Kunhardt et al 1995).

The stereopticon was a slide projector or "magic lantern," dating back to the mid 19th century, and was a popular form of entertainment and education. The Americans, William and Frederick Langenheim, introduced the stereopticon slide technology— projecting photographs on glass—in 1850, charging a fee of ten cents. One could view realistic photographs with nature, history, and science themes.

During the winter of 1882-1883, the five Ringling brothers, Al, Otto, Alf. T, Charles, and John, ages 16-30, put on a variety show in Baraboo, Wisconsin (Chindahl 1959).

In 1884, a "white" (albino) elephant was brought by Barnum for his exhibition. Forepaugh exhibited a fake white elephant (Chindahl 1959).

In the spring of the same year, 1884, the Ringling Brothers talked with a retired circus owner, Yankee Robinson (Fayette Ludovic Robinson), and organized *Yankee Robinson's Great Show, Ringling Brothers' Carnival of Novelties, and Denar's Museum of Living Wonders*, transported by nine wagons not counting the privilege wagons which were for such things as sideshows, concessions, and games, run by individuals who bought the "privilege" from the circus owners. The Ringling Brothers bought a "Big Top," (90 x 45 feet) and a smaller tent for the sideshow, first performance was 19 May 1884. In the next year they toured as *Ringling Bros.' Great Double Shows, Circus, Caravan, and Trained Animal Exposition* with 12 wagons (Chindahl 1959, ICHF n.d., Culhane 1991, North and Hatch 1960). North and Hatch (1960) stated they started with "twenty-two horse and nine wagons, not counting the "Privilege Wagons." By 1885 they had fifteen wagons and a big top eighty feet in diameter which is slightly smaller "Big Top" than other authors reported.

There were 14 traveling shows in 1884 (Culhane 1991).

In 1885 the *Ringling Bros.' Great Double Shows, Circus, Caravan, and Trained Animal Exposition* toured with twelve wagons and wagons for the sideshow and other privilege wagons. The Sells Bros. Circus, *Sells Brothers' Quadruple Alliance, Museum, Menagerie, Caravan and Circus,* toured 1862 -1863, and 1871-1895. (Chindahl 1959).

In St. Thomas, Ontario, Canada, many rail lines converged. The circus trains stopped near the middle and forward part so the animals would have a rather short walk to the circus grounds. Before the circus prepared for their next move, Fred R. Armes, operator in charge of the Grand Trunk Railroad depot, apparently warned the elephant handlers not to load until after the westbound express freight passed through. However the elephant handlers decided to ignore this advice. They removed a portion of the right-of-way fence and marched twenty-nine elephants up the embankment, across the main track, and into their cars. Then as soon as their act finished, they led Jumbo and a smaller elephant down the track toward Jumbo's boxcar. The Grand Trunk's Special Freight #151 entered the yards and gathered speed on the downgrade. Matthew Scott tried to lead the two elephants away from the approaching train and down the embankment, but the elephants wouldn't go that way. Scott turned away but Jumbo was hit by the engine and shoved under the heavy wheeled carriage of a circus wagon which crushed his skull. Shortly thereafter Barnum wrote a version on the event in which he claimed that Jumbo snatched and hurled the smaller elephant off the track and faced the approaching locomotive, meeting death with a becoming dignity and fortitude. It became the widely accepted version of Jumbo's death (Culhane 1991, Kunhardt et al 1995).

At the end of the 1885 season, Bailey sold his share of the circus to James E. Cooper and W. Cole (Chindahl 1959).

For their 1886 tour the Ringling Brothers had the *Ringling Bros. Great Double Shows and Congress of Wild and Trained Animals,* with a ninety-foot round top and eighteen wagons in addition to 2 cages, a Ticket, and a Band Wagon. Their menagerie had a hyena, a bear, monkeys, and an eagle. The show became in 1887 *Ringling Bros. United Monster Shows, Great Double Circus, Royal European Menagerie, Museum, Caravan and Congress of Trained Animals.* All the new wagons, cages, chariots and band wagons were built by the Moeller Brothers, their cousins, at the Moeller Wagon and Buggy Works in Baraboo, Wisconsin (North and Hatch 1960, Dewel 1998). Other companies that built wagons for the circuses were: Sebastian Manufacturing Company, the Fielding Brothers, and John Stephenson, all of New York, and Bode Wagon Co. of Cincinnati, Ohio (Kathleen 2019).

The style of circus bandwagons was entirely different from village bandwagons. Circus bandwagons were often called tableau bandwagons due to the elaborate carvings on their sides. They were intended to be gaudy. The musicians sat at a considerable height. Usually there were compartments under the floor for storage of the instruments (Kathleen 2019).

By 1888 Bailey bought the interests of Cooper, Cole, and Hutchinson, and now called the circus *Barnum & Bailey's Greatest Show on Earth*. The circus used three rings, two stages, and a hippodrome track (Chindahl 1959).

The Ringling Brothers leased the Van Amburgh title and toured in 1889 as the *Ringling Bros. and Van Amburgh's United Monster Circus, Museum, Menagerie, Roman Hippodrome and Universal World's Exposition*. Management of things were handled by vaious Ringlings: Albert, equestrian director (the producer and director of the whole show); Charles, general manager (commanded the logistics of moving everything from one place to another); Otto, financial management; Alf T., public relations; and, John, routing (Chindahl 1959, Culhane 1991, North and Hatch 1960).

In1888 they added a new Big Top (100 x 148 feet), a menagerie, three horse tops, a dressing top, bought two elephants, two camels, an emu, and something they called a "Zebue" as they expanded their circus (North and Hatch 1960).

The *Adam Forepaugh Circus* was the first to integrate a Wild West Show into its Big Top program, a tradition that continued into the early twentieth century.

In 1889, James A. Bailey and James E. Cooper bought Forepaugh's circus, enlarged it, and toured the Pacific Coast in 1891. Forepaugh sold his railroad cars to the Ringling Brothers. Much of the (Forepaugh) equipment went over to the Cody's *Buffalo Bill Wild West* show per the agreement between James A. Bailey and the partnership of Cody and Salisbury. The Ringlings used the equipment to transform their circus from a small animal-powered production to a huge rail-powered behemoth, which later purchased the Barnum & Bailey Circus. In liquidating his circus assets,

Forepaugh indirectly contributed to the demise of his arch-rival. The Ringlings began traveling by rail at the start of the 1890 season (Culhane 1991).

Forepaugh died in 1890. Cooper died in 1892. Bailey bought Cooper's share and assigned it to Joseph T. McCaddon (Cooper's brother-in-law). That show discontinued at the end of 1894 (Chindahl 1959).

Barnum & Bailey's Greatest Show on Earth toured the eastern states and parts of Quebec in 1889 (Chindahl 1959).

By 1890 there were more miles of railroad track in the United States than all of Europe, including Russia (Culhane 1991).

The Ringling Brothers opened their first railroad show on 2 May 1890, in Baraboo, Wisconsin (North and Hatch 1960). They had two advertising cars (sent ahead of the main train), one performers' sleeper (for 54 performers), one elephant car (3 elephants), five stockcars, and eight flat cars carrying 2 tableau wagons, 2 band wagons, 15 cages (with 2 open dens), 107 horses, 3 camels, 4 lions, 2 lion cubs, 1 hippopotamus, and other animals.

In 1890 twenty five traveling shows were moving around in the United States. In the same year Horace Frederick Miltemore (stage name Fred Fisher), of Bloomington, Illinois, invented the flying return act, introduced in the *King & Franklin Circus* by Miltemore and Charles Noble (stage name Charles Fisher). The rigging consisted of a pedestal and long trapeze at one end and, a short trapeze at the other end. The rigging was about 40 feet from the pedestal board to the catcher, usually 32 - 36 feet in the air. One flyer stands on the narrow platform, swings off his trapeze, the flybar, and is caught by the other aerialist, the catcher, swinging by his hocks from the other trapeze. The two complete their swing and the flyer is returned to the pedestal board by way of the flybar. It was felt that a safety device, a net, should be deployed. It was built by a Pekin, Illinois, fisherman. The act was initially performed by The Fisher Brothers, naming themselves after the net maker (Cole 2007, Gossard 1999, Parkinson 1956, Chindahl 1959, Culhane 1991, Summers 2018).

In 1900, the *Ringling Bros. World's Greatest Shows* listed most of their female performers as Miss: Miss Minnie Fisher {iron jaw act}; Miss Nettie Carroll {slack wire}; Miss Jessie Leon {wire walking}; Miss Belle Carmen {high wire}, Miss Lizzie Rooney, Miss Elena Rayland, and Miss Emeline Fredericks {equestrians}; Miss Ida Miaco {hand-balancing and contortion}; Miss Allies Jackson; Miss Minnie Johnson; and, Madame Noble {horsewoman} (Reid 2010).

There were around a hundred shows in 1890, but the numbers were greatly reduced by the depression of 1893. (Hoh and Rough 1990).

The *Gollmar Bros. Greatest of American Shows* operated out of winter quarters on Baraboo's Second Avenue from 1891, with a moderate sized overland wagon circus, until 1916, with brothers Walter, Fred, Charles, Ben, and Jake Gollmar as proprietors. (Circus Historical Society, Inc. 2020)

Bailey bought Barnum's share of the circus from Barnum's widow short after Barnum died, 7 April 1891, at the age of eighty (Chindahl 1959, Culhane 1991).

By 1891 the Ringling Brothers traveled with 22 railroad cars: two for advertising staff, three sleepers, eleven flat cars, five stock cars, and one elephant car (Culhane 1991).

In 1891 there were seven circuses traveling by rail. The Ringling Brothers named their show the *Ringling Bros. World's Greatest Railroad Shows, Real Roman Hippodrome, 3 Ring Circus and Elevated Stages, Millionaire Menagerie, Museum and Aquarium and Spectacular Tournament Production of Caeser's Triumphal Entry in Rome.* This type of humbug was a real Barnum moment (Hoh and Rough 1990, North and Hatch 1960).

1892 was a bad year for the Ringling Brothers in terms of their railroad operations. During a rain near Washington, Kansas, on 17 May, there was a crash where four stock cars were demolished, 26 horses killed or put down from injuries, and 2 men killed and 4 seriously injured. A second crash was near Centralia, Missouri, on 18 September, with six cages demolished and, a little marring on the sleeping cars, but no one injured. The third crash was at Centralia, Illinois, where the train had a rear end collision with no damage other than "a few broken irons on the cars" (North and Hatch 1960).

In the same year Charles and Alf T. Ringling decided to build a bell wagon. Three Wisconsin businesses were selected: one firm furnishing the bells and their supports; one constructing the wagon; and, the third supplying the carvings to decorate the vehicle. The bells were cast by Campbell, Gardiner & Sons, a bell and iron foundry and machine shop at 238-256 Oregon Street, Milwaukee, Wisconsin. They ran from nineteen to thirty six inches in diameter (bottom) and from fifteen to twenty eight inches (to the top). The bells were rung by a clapper activated by a lever on the rear mounted console. The carvings on the side were supplied by the Milwaukee Ornamental Carving Co. The largest bell weighed about 1 ton. Because the narrow, iron-shod wheels would sink on any muddy circus lot, they maintained a fifty-horse hitch in case they needed to pull it free (Dahlinger 1984, North and Hatch 1960).

Expositions happened in various places in the world

at various time. They were intended to showcase the achievements of the host nation.

The 1893 World's Columbian Exposition in Chicago (630 acres) celebrated the 100th anniversary of Christopher Columbus (one year late). During the six months of its existence it had an estimated 27 million visitors. Chicago at that time had a population of just over 1 million. It displayed more than a million artifacts from many countries. It had a Midway Plaisance, approximately 12 city blocks of linear parkway, which was about 1 mile long , with living displays of various cultures (essentially a human menagerie), bazaars, food offerings, and rides, very much the essence of past circuses.

Frederick W. Putnam, the second director of Harvard's Peabody Museum, was the supervisor of anthropology at the fair. Franz Boas, often called the father of anthropology in the United States, worked with him in the design and construction of the cultural exhibits. This was the first time that anthropology had been recognized at such a level in the United States (Jacknis 2019,).

Various authors have suggested that the Midway began the development of carnivals.

The planers wished to have something to rival the Eiffel Tower. George Washington Ferris, Jr., built a 255-foot diameter wheel mounted on a 71-ton axle, the largest hollow forged piece ever built at that time. It was somewhat shorter than the Eiffel Tower which is 1,063 feet tall, about the same height as an 81-storey building. The wheel carried 36 cars, each capable of holding 40 people with more than 1.4 million people paying 50 cents for a 20-minute ride. The cars were 27 feet long, 13 feet wide, and 9 feet tall, hung from a 6 ½ inch diameter iron axle, and had revolving chairs (Malanowski

2015, Anderson 1992).

After the exposition closed Otto Schmitt, one of the showman, formed the *Chicago Midway Plaisance Amusement Company,* with thirteen acts, including some from the World's Fair, and began a tour of the northeast United States. His company closed due to poor management practices, before completing its first tour (Smith 2016).

William Washington Cole sold his show (a medium-sized American circus founded in1884 as *W.W. Cole's New Colossal Shows*) at auction in 1896, and purchased an interest in Barnum's enterprise and accepted an executive position with the Barnum & Bailey organization The circus tent was a 252-foot round top with four 59-foot middle pieces, overall that main tent was 252 x 488 feet. Bailey changed the name to the *Great Adam Forepaugh and Sells Bros.' Shows Combined.* He now controlled three large shows: the *Barnum & Bailey, Buffalo Bill's Wild West,* and *the Forepaugh-Sells.* (Chindhal 1959, Culhane 1991).

The Edison organization presented the first movie projector, the cinematograph, in New York in 1896. The next year, 1897, Ringling Brothers toured with one in a black tent as an annex show (Culhane 1991).

The Ringling Brothers added to their 1897 circus parades with thirty mounted musicians on pure-white horses with highly polished musical instruments and red-plumed helmets (North and Hatch 1960).

From 1897 to 1902 Bailey had the Barnum circus on tour in Europe. In 1902, once back in the U.S., Bailey enlarged the circus to the point that it took around ninety railroad cars to haul it from place to place. (Chindahl 1959).

The horse was still the primary means of transportation. Most knew horses from long acquaintance and enjoyed watching superior riders doing things with them (Cluhane 1991).

In the years 1900, 1903, 1904, and 1905, the Ringling Brothers toured widely including the west coast, Montreal, and various of the states, making their first round-trip in 1900, exhibiting in every section of the country (Chindahl 1959).

In 1903 Bailey once again utilized the forty-horse hitch connected to the largest, heaviest, and most ornate wagon ever constructed, the *Two Hemispheres* bandwagon. It was 30 feet long, 8½ feet wide, 12 feet tall and weighed more than 6.5 tons. It was built by the Sebastian Wagon Co., New York, for $4,400. It had gilt carvings of lions crouching next to globes, one side the Eastern Hemisphere, the other side the Western Hemisphere, as well as carvings of classic circus animals, scrolls, and the national seals of 12 countries (Culhane 1991, Willard 2001).

Bailey and associates and the Ringling Brothers agreed (again) upon a division of territory for their operations in 1904. On 10 January 1905, Bailey transferred a half-interest of the Forepaugh-Sells show to the Ringling Brothers (Chindahl 1959).

In 1903, the *Gollmar Bros. Circus* changed to railroad travel. At its peak the show used up to 22 rail cars. It was a major circus in the mid-west. They added a couple ornate wagons to their street parade. Ben Gollmar built the body and designed the layout of the sides and the carvings for the sides. That wagon was the Band Wagon carrying a 15-member band from 1903 through 1916 (Circus Historical Society, Inc. 2020).

In 1904 a power-driven stake driver mounted on a wagon, driven by a four-horsepower gasoline engine, was utilized by the Ringling Brothers (Chindahl 1959).

The Ringling Brothers began to use the rail system traveling on forty-four cars in 1895. For the first time they traveled in New England, competing with Barnum & Bailey. Bailey suggested that they agree to divide the United States with him. Each was assigned a particular geographical area: the Barnum circus was given the West, the Ringlings the East, and Forepaugh-Sells the North and South (Chindahl 1959, Montgomery and McCullough 2013).

The Barnum & Bailey show toured the west coast in 1905. In San Francisco, on the hippodrome track under the tent they paraded 260 draft horses, four abreast (Chindahl 1959).

Bailey died at age fifty-eight in 1906. Direction was then given to George O. Starr who worked for the corporation *Barnum & Bailey, Limited* (Chindahl 1959).

The 1906 tour went to through New Brunswick, Quebec and Ontario, Canada. W. W. Cole and J. T. McCaddon were elected members of the board of directors, 23 November 1906. Cole was appointed to succeed Starr as the manager of the: *Barnum & Bailey Circus,* and the *Buffalo Bill Wild West Show* (Chindahl 1959).

During October 1907 the Barnum & Bailey show was sold to the Ringling Brothers for $410,000. The English stockholders met and ratified the sale of the American property by Mrs. Bailey (New York Times 1907, Hoff 1907). The Stock Certificates of the Barnum & Bailey Limited were issued in 1902, by The Commercial Bank of Scotland - Edinburgh England. Most of the shares were turned in when the company was sold to the Ringling Brothers (Scripophily n.d.).

In1908 the Ringling Brothers made enough profit to cover the price that they had paid Mrs. Bailey (Jensen

1975).

The Ringling Brothers on 29 December 1910, met in Chicago with representatives of the twelve largest shows to form an association of circus owners with a constitution and bylaws, membership open to all circuses and wild west shows. It disbanded after a few months due to a lack of co-operation among the members (Chindahl 1959).

On 21 May 1910, the *Barnum & Bailey Circus* Big Top burned, with no injuries, at Schenectady, New York (Chindahl 1959).

There were more than thirty circuses traveling around in 1910, in 1911 there were thirty-two (Chindahl 1959, Hoh and Rough 1990).

In 1910 the *Gollmar Brothers Greatest of American Shows* had a general renovation of all its tents. They also bought for $6,500, a giant hippopotamus. (Circus Historical Society, Inc. 2020, Watertown Historical Society 2020).

The *Forepaugh-Sells Circus* closed after the death of Otto Ringling on 31 March 1911. This left two large circuses: The *Ringling Brother Circus*, and the *Barnum & Bailey Circus* (Chindahl 1959, Culhane 1991).

The *Gollmar Brothers Greatest of American Shows* sold over 3,000 tickets to a matinee performance - in a town, Monona, Iowa, of 875 people (Jarmes n.d.).

In 1912 the Ringling Brothers introduced a new equestrian act acclaimed to be the finest equestrian in the world, May Wirth. She was the most adept trick rider that had appeared in the equestrian ring and became the most well known person of her time. On 22 August, while the circus was at Sterling Illinois, the Big Top burned with no serious injury to anyone (Chindahl 1959, Culhane 1991).

In 1913 the electric lights previously utilized by the

Barnum & Bailey circuses were replaced with two wagons carrying 25-kilowatt 125-volt direct current generators connected to a four-cylinder, four cycle 560 RPM gasoline engine to run the lights (Chindahl 1959).

In 1914 John Ringling staged a ballet of eighty ballerinas, beginning to again merge theater and circus productions (North and Hatch 1960).

The use of a tractor to supplement the draft horses was used by the *Sells-Floto Circus*. More tractors were added in 1916 to raise center poles, canvas tops and to load and unload the canvas. The circus with three rings, two stages, and eight center poles traveled across the United States in 1916 (Chindahl 1959).

The *Gollmar Brothers Circus* was sold in 1917 to carnival owner, James Patterson and renamed the *Patterson-Gollmar Bros. Circus*. (Circus Historical Society, Inc. 2020)

By 1917 the Ringling Brothers circus had 1,000 personnel, 335 horses, 26 elephants, 16 camels, and traveled by rail with 92 railroad cars. During the First World War they had major problems in filling positions: 80 canvasmen instead of 250, 20 property men instead of 80. The global influenza epidemic claimed twenty-two million people in the United States. The railroads stated that they could not longer support two big circuses. In 1918 they closed their season early and moved the Ringling Brothers circus to Bridgeport, Wisconsin, where their Barnum & Bailey circus wintered over having decided that they had to combine the two into one. They did this by combining the *Ringling Bros.' World's Greatest Show* and the *Barnum & Bailey's Greatest Show on Earth* into the *Ringling Bros. and Barnum & Bailey Combined Shows* (ninety-nine rail cars). This signaled the end of Baraboo as a circus town (Culhane 1991, Chindahl 1959, North and Hatch 1960).

During the winter of 1918-1919, two of the Ringling Brother worked on the planning required to fit 168 different acts into the overall performance of their circus. They now had a six pole Big Top (North and Hatch 1960) as their show was becoming bigger and bigger.

John Ringling decided to no longer utilize Madison Square Garden as it was too small for the Ringling Brothers circus. He associated with George Lewis "Tex" Rickard, a promoter of sporting events. Ringling formed the New Madison Square Corporation, as chairman of the board and its largest stock holder. The new building, at 49th Street and Eighth Avenue, costing $5.6 million, was built in 249 days, overseen by Rickard and architect Thomas Lamb. It held an 18,000-seat arena and opened with a six-day bicycle race on 24 November 1925.

The *Blueshirts* were granted a National Hockey League franchise prior to the 1926-1927 season. This new team, which played in the new building became known in the press as "Tex's Rangers" after Rickard's nickname. The team soon dropped the *Tex* and became known as the *Rangers* (NHL 2016). Rickard died from appendicitis on 6 January 1929.

Ringling Brothers-Barnum & Bailey Circus opened 1926 (North and Hatch1960, NHL 2016).

The *Ringling-Barnum & Bailey Circus* opened in 1927 with a Grand Entry and acts in three rings and two stages (Chindahl 1959).

The decision was made to move in 1927 the circus winter quarters from Bridgeport to Sarasota, Florida. The land in Florida was relatively cheap, the climate was warm, which lowered the winter heating costs, and, John Ringling liked that area. The outdoor practice area for the performers was as large as the New Madison Square Garden arena. It allowed the circus to charge visitors if they wanted to watch (North and Hatch 1960).

In 1929 it was time to renegotiate the circus contract with Madison Square Garden for the next season. John Ringling did not come as he was in a debate with them about scheduling. The Garden Management gave the contract to the *American Circus Corporation*. It had been organized in 1921 by Jerry Mugivan, Bert Powers and Edward Ballard to enlarge their circus holdings. John Ringling bought the *American Circus Corporation* for around $ 2,000,000, adding an additional 150 railroad cars, 2,000 animals, tents, baggage stock, and 4,500 people This put Ringling in charge of all the large circuses in America. The big top was now 200-feet in diameter with five forty-foot middle pieces (Chindahl 1959, North and Hatch 1960).

The depression started in 1929. The number of circuses as railroad shows, began to dwindle: 1929 -13; 1930 - 11; 1931 - 8; 1932 - 4; 1933-1935 - 3; 1936-1937 - 4; 1938 -2; 1939 -1943 -2; 1944 - 3; 1945 -6; 1946 - 4; 1947 - 5; 1948-1950 - 4. By the close of 1956 there were no longer railroad shows (Chindahl 1959).

In 1931 the circus added Clyde Beatty to present his animal act after five years of not having this type of act (Chindahl 1959).

In 1932, *Ringling Brothers-Barnum & Bailey Combined Shows, Incorporated* was formed in Wilmington, Delaware, to keep the operation from economic collapse (North and Hatch 1960).

The menagerie tent, in 1937, contained 21 cage wagons (Chindahl 1959).

The circus made a 27-state tour in 1939, traveling 17,117 miles. Air-cooling apparatus was mounted on 8 wagons spaced around the side walls to cool the interior of the main tent. Draft horses were discarded as trucks became common, reducing the number of stock cars, employees, the number of workingmen's sleepers, and the eliminated the baggage-stock tent, among other changes (Chindahl 1959, North and Hatch 1960).

Fire destroyed the menagerie tent in 1942 and killed 39 animals (Chindahl 1959).

Disaster struck the circus on 6 July 1944, when the Big Top burned during a matinee in Hardford, Connecticut with 168 deaths and hundreds of other people burned as well as 50-60 circus employees. $3,946,335.70 were paid out in claims driving the circus into receivership. By December 1950 all the claims were paid by the insurance carried by the circus and the earnings of the circus (Chindhal 1959).

The Greatest Show On Earth traveled on four trains in 1941 with 107, 6-foot long cages and freight wagons (Johnson 1990).

By 1946 all the canvas utilized for tents by the circus was flameproof. They began to mechanize many of the construction aspects of erecting the main tent in 1948. Aluminum side poles and quarter poles replaced wooden ones with a weight reduction of 50%. Seats (about 220) and bleachers, were erected from trucks, using the power takeoff on a Jeep, whose systems set up and spread out these facilities. The grandstand was supported by the main frames of trucks having 16 wing jacks for support. Steel cables and winches were used for hoisting various other aspects of the big tent. The cookhouse was modernized to resemble the big hotels equipment of steam kettles, dishwashers, etc. In many ways this reduced the need for the previous manpower, reducing the overhead cost of the circus. The kitchen was producing 4,000 meals a day using: 2,000 pounds of meat,

1,500 loaves of bread, 2,800 eggs, 5,000 pancakes, and 1,000 quarts of milk. The cost of these supplies had doubled by this time. The railroad charged for hauling for four long trains was $180,000 in 1941 and $580,000 in 1955. Daily expenses were over $25,000 a day (Chindahl 1959, North and Hatch 1960).

In 1949 they took a one-ring European-style circus to Havana during the winter to help defray the cost of maintaining their winter quarters in Florida. A costume factory was set up in Sarasota as a cost cutting measure (North and Hatch 1960).

Ringling Brothers and Barnum and Bailey Circus had in 1955, the largest number of elephants in a single circus, 50 (Johnson 1990).

By 1956, they realized that the road show had to go. It now took a fifteen acre lot to hold the forty-one tents in which the circus lived and performed. It took another lot to hold 3,000 parked cars. There was not any space that large near the urban centers as those centers were spreading out. Between 1860 and 1900, the number of urban-dwellers had gone from five million to twenty-five million. At 11:15 p.m. on 16 July 1956, the Big Top came down for the last time (North and Hatch 1960, Bogdan 1988).

The Ringlings analyzed their circus (North and Hatch 1960). They had:

The railroad business, moving 67,000 tons of equipment, animals, and people, 20,000 miles a year.

A restaurant business, serving at least 900,000 meals a year.

A hotel business, providing sleeping accommodations for 1,300 people for eight months.

A construction business, building an amphitheater and
tented town every day or so.

The only activity that brought in any money was show
business. The rest had to go.

They cut the sideshow and the menagerie, but kept the
performing animals.

Instead of an eighty-car train, they would use three
baggage cars in which the elephants and other trained
animals would ride.

The smaller trained animals would travel in motor
vans.

The physical equipment of the show – rigging,
properties, and costumes – were to move in ten trailer trucks.

Performers would get travel allowances but use their
own transportation, mostly cars and trailers, and live and eat
in restaurants and hotels of their choice.

Arthur Concello, General Manager, designed a new
type of aerial rigging which could be assembled and
interlocked to the ground, and hoisted aloft by a single-cable
action. It could be raised in ball parks, outdoor venues, and
inside buildings to the ceilings.

☞ The Midway ☜

The Midway, in America, was an extra, secondary production associated with a circus, carnival, fair, or some other such attraction.

The midway was the amusement area, sideshows, refreshment stands, etc., between the main ticket booth and the entrance to the big top, literally "midway" between the two.

The concept was P. T. Barnum's.

The Sideshows

The Sideshows were usually housed in a separate and smaller tent located on the midway of a circus with two basic types of sideshow acts: *Working Acts* and *Human Oddities*. They were created to entertain audiences waiting for the big show performance and to generate additional revenue.

Sideshows are unique to American circuses. These acts were presented close to the audience, acts that would be lost in the overall performances exhibited in the center ring of the big top. (Anon n.d.2). Tickets were sold separately from the main event and considered as a "side attraction" which morphed into "sideshow."

Human Oddities, or as it was frequently labeled, *The Freak Show*, started with Barnum long before there was something called The Sideshow. *Freaks* was not a quality that belonged to the person on display, it was something created, a perspective, a set of practices, a social construct (Bogdan 1988).

A term often used was *lusus naturae*, Latin for "a sport of nature; freak of nature." This gave the label a more quasi-academic tone.

Hornberger (2005) wrote:

> Human curiosities have been around as long as there have been human beings, and the general public has always been fascinated by them.

> This fascination really exploded into high gear in the mid-1880s. With the industrial revolution in full swing, people found themselves having plenty of something they never had before: leisure time.
> One of the first, and certainly the most famous, individuals to capitalize on this was Phineas Taylor Barnum.

Crockett (2014) wrote:

> In 19th century America, gawking at people who were born with deformities was not only socially acceptable -- it was considered family entertainment.

Barnum, in 1834, began to exhibit Joice Heth, an elderly slave. He bought her from R.W. Lindsay, a promoter, from Kentucky. The agreement sold her for the remainder of the twelve months that Lindsay had the right to exhibit her. Barnum paid $1,000 and earned $1,500 every week from his show. Heth had been exhibited by others with little success. Barnum brought her to New York, advertised her as the "Greatest natural and national curiosity" of the day with an age of 161, that she had been nurse maid to the young George

Washington. The first half of the 19th century saw the acceleration and culmination of a process by which the "Father of His Country" was virtually deified — the greatest American of all time, with more than 400 books, essays, and other writings between 1800 and 1860. Barnum and his partner, Levi Lyman, starting in 1835, exhibited Heth across the northeast for seven months in taverns, inns, museums, railway houses, and concert halls. Joice Heth became a popular subject in the pages of the "three-penny press" (often called the penny press), which catered to urban working-class readers and challenged the cultural authority of more genteel (and more expensive, at six cents per copy) newspapers. When ticket sales tapered off, Barnum wrote an anonymous letter to a Boston newspaper claiming that Heth was a fake -- that she was actually a machine, made up of whale bone and old leather. Crowds flocked again to see her. Heth died of natural causes in 1836. Although a prominent doctor performed an autopsy and concluded that Heth was no more than 80, Barnum countered that the corpse was a fake and continued to claim that Heth was still alive and performing elsewhere (The Lost Museum Archive 2020, Reiss 1999, Crockett 2014, John 1990).).

Barnum began to master the art of colorful trickery in 1842 with the *Feejee Mermaid* as a "creature with the head of a monkey and the tail of a fish." It was actually the torso and head of a juvenile monkey sewn to the back half of a fish, apparently sold to an Englishman by Japanese sailors in 1822, for $6,000 ($103,500 today). In New York, he negotiated to lease it from the Boston Museum for $12.50 per week. He told a story about the mermaid's discovery to newspapers and distributed 10,000+ pamphlets, resulting within weeks of a high public interest/curiosity (Crockett 2014).

Barnum in his museums (1842-1865, 1866-1868) and his circus activities (1851-1853) apparently decided from his experience with the Joice Heth show there was an audience for what he called "Marvelous Living Human Curiosities." He started with "midgets" (American Heritage 1966).

The term "midget" was used by Harriet Beecher Stowe in *Sunny Memories of Foreign Lands and Old Town Folks* where she described children and an extremely short man. Barnum featured General Tom Thumb, Lavinia Warren, and Commodore Nutt in his circus which helped the term to become popularized. It became linked to referencing short people put on public display for curiosity and sport although Barnum elevated them to positions of high society with fantasy military titles.

"Midget" and "Dwarf" became commons terms during this time, with the usage suggesting that midgets were small, but perfectly formed, while dwarf had a normal upper body, but deformed lower limbs. The word "midget" was never coined as the official term to identify people with dwarfism, but was created as a label used to refer to people of short stature who were on public display for curiosity and sport. Today (2015), the word "midget" is considered a derogatory slur (Culhane 1990, LPA 2015).

The sideshow, the freak show, became an integral part of the circus (Bogdan 1988).

Barnum started in 1842 with Charles S. Stratton who was 25 inches tall and weighed 15 pounds, described by Barnum as "a perfectly formed bright-eyed fellow, with light hair and ruddy cheeks and he enjoyed the best of health." Barnum made a deal with his father, Sherwood E. Stratton, for four weeks, $3.00 a week, and paying all traveling and boarding charges for the boy and his mother. Barnum advertised "General Tom Thumb, a dwarf of eleven years of age, just arrived from England." He apparently borrowed the name from the legend of King Arthur where one of the characters was named Sir Tom Thumb. Tom Thumb wore a Revolutionary War soldier's uniform and had been taught to sing, dance, and impersonate famous figures (Cupid, Napoleon Bonaparte). At the end of the four weeks, Barnum made a contract for $7.00 a week, plus a bonus at the end of $50.00. Before the year was out the weekly salary rose to $25.00 and by 1844 to $50.00 a week.

In 1862 Tom married Lavinia Warren, another small person. This event was so popularized that Queen Victoria sent wedding presents to them. Tom retired at the age of 20 (Hornberger 2005, Culhane 1990, Crockett 2014).

In 1847, after touring Europe, Barnum returned to the United States and toured the cities of the east and numbers of New England towns. The crowds were larger than Barnum's Museum had ever seen. President Polk and his wife had them visit (Culhane 1990).

His museum offered *Marvellous Living Human Curiosities* {spelling as written as that time}.

Chang and Eng, connected by a four-inch ligament at the chest, were born in 1811. A British merchant, Robert Hunter, and his partner, Abel Coffin, established a contract with the twins {variously reported as $500 dollars, or $3,000 dollars}, and exhibited them around Europe and America in the late 1820s for three years.

Tracey wrote (1927):

> One day when the twins were 18 years old, a Yankee skipper dropped anchor in the harbor and accidentally met the Twins. He immediately shanghaied them and brought

them to Boston. They created a sensation, not only around Boston but in Europe where their protector next journeyed with them.

One account states that the term *Siamese Twins* was created by a doctor who witnessed the two perform, so named because they were born in a small Siamese fishing village. Another account states that Coffin called them *Siamese Double Boys*. After a long career elsewhere, in 1850, they signed a contract to tour with P.T. Barnum. For the next twenty years, they intermittently performed. They died four hours apart in 1879, leaving a great fortune to their wives (Hornberger 2005, Crockett 2014).

Jennie Quigley was born in 1850, in Glasgow, Scotland, the daughter of James Quigley and Jane Kerr Quigley. She moved to Brooklyn, New York with her mother and brother in 1861. In 1863 Barnum billed her as *The Queen of Scotland* and *The Smallest Lady in the World*. She was under two feet tall, and grew to 36 inches when she was 28. She retired in 1917, 41 inches tall.

The *Bearded Lady* became a cliché, a staple of a carnival freak show.

Josephine Clofullia (née Boisdechêne) born near Geneva, Switzerland, around 1830, started sprouting facial hair in childhood, likely the result of hypertrichosis. The late-adolescent Boisdechêne began performing to help make ends meet when her family fell on hard times, By 1853, Boisdechêne, a married mother, now known as "Madame Clofullia," came to the United States and joined Barnum's show where she was known as *The Bearded Lady of Geneva*. However Barnum felt that she was not drawing sufficient numbers. He had William Chaar sue him for false advertising.

The case was heard by a New York City magistrate on 1 July 1853. Barnum introduced testimony from Madame Clofullia's father and husband, as well as from three physicians, each of whom had examined Clofullia. The case was dismissed: Clofullia, the judge ruled, was indeed a woman. Barnum hoped, that a torrent of spectators would rush to the museum to look and decide for themselves. The case had been widely reported in the press (Trainor 2015, American Heritage 1966).

In 1857 Barnum was in Europe and stopped at the Amsterdam Fair. There he saw the albino Lucasie Family, probably French. He convinced them to come with him to be part of his museum. He claimed that they were "Negroes from Madagascar" and that they slept with their eyes open (Trav 2012).

On 24 November 1859 Charles Darwin's book, *On The Origin of Species by Means of Natural Selection, Or the Preservation of Favoured Races in the Struggle For Life*, was published. 1,500 copies sold out the first day. A second edition was released in England and the United States.

Three months later, in 1860 Barnum recruited William Henry Johnson, born, in 1842 in New Jersey, in an impoverished, newly-freed slave family. His head was slightly microcephalic, or cone-shaped. Barnum named him "Zip," a "different race of human found during a gorilla trekking expedition near the Gambia River in western Africa." With a shaved head and dressed in a head-to-toe fur suit he was promoted as a "missing link" or "The What Is it," or "Man-Monkey." Johnson, displayed in a cage, was only supposed to grunt. He was paid $1.00 a day" for his performance.   Eventually Barnum paid him $100 per performance, often 10 per week, and purchased him a lavish home in Connecticut. Zip was frugal and retired a millionaire

(Crockett 2014, Kundardt et al 1995, Culhane 1990, Bogdan 1988, Hornberger 2005, Hartzman 2005).

Lavinia Warren, born in 1841 in Middleboro, Massachusetts, was 32 inches tall, and weighed 29 pounds by her tenth birthday. Barnum convinced her to join his show in 1861, paying $1,000 a week. Barnum spent as much as $2,000 per outfit for her (Hornberger 2005, Kunhardt et al 1995).

Zalumma Agra, was called the Star of the East, a Circassian Beauty.

She was a young local with frizzy hair attired in Turkish garb with commentary for the visitors that was the usual mixture of science, graphic slave-auction detail, and the erotic suggestion of harem life. She was followed by a number of "imports" whose first name started with "Z" (Kunhardt et al 1995).

The New York Daily Times (1856) wrote:

> . . . this traffic in white slaves will be over, the Circassian dealers have redoubled their efforts ever since the commencement of the peace conferences to introduce into Turkey the greatest possible number of women while the opportunity of doing so lasted. They have been so successful, notwithstanding the prohibition of the trade by the Porte, and the presence of so many of Her Majesty's ships in the Black Sea, that never, perhaps, at any former period, was white human flesh so cheap as it is at this moment. There is an absolute glut in the market, and dealers are obliged to throw away their goods, owing to the extent of the supply, which in many instances has been brought by

steam under the British flag. In former times a "good middling" Circassian girl was thought very cheap at 100 pounds, but at the present moment the same description of goods may be had for 5 pounds!

With low prices a low class of purchasers come into the market. Formerly a Circassian slave girl was pretty sure of being bought into a good family, where not only good treatment, but often rank and fortune awaited her; but at present low rates she may be taken by any huxter who never thought of keeping a slave before. Another evil is that the temptation to possess a Circassian girl at such low prices is so great in the minds of the Turks that many who cannot afford to keep several slaves have been sending their blacks to market, in order to make room for a newly-purchased white girl.

Butchart (n.d.) wrote {spelling in original}:

America found itself in the midst of a Civil War dominated by ideologies of enslavement and freedom. It was at this point that showman and future circus impresario PT Barnum stepped in, ever keen to capitalise on exotic tales of savagery and captivity, using the harem as the epitome of the Orientalist fantasy. From Barnum's correspondence it becomes clear that accepted ideas about the Circassian 'beautiful white slave girl' were paramount in his decision to add them to his roster. He wrote in a letter to his procurer;

'I still have faith in a beautiful Circassian girl if you can get one very beautiful [...] or if you can hire one or two at reasonable prices, do so if you think they are pretty and will pass for Circassian slaves [...] If you don't find one that is beautiful & possesses a striking kind of beauty, why of course she won't draw and you must give it up as a bad job.

With Barnum re-casting the Circassian Beauty for an American audience he was playing into contemporary debates that raged around freedom and slavery. His first Circassian Beauty, Zalumma Agra 'the star of the east', went on display in 1864 – during the Civil War – and became the prototype for an act that remained a feature of the sideshow for nearly fifty years.

The Circassian Beauty was constructed by Barnum as an embodiment of the seductive qualities of the harem, and as such her garments was paramount. She wore baggy Turkish-style trousers with revealing flowing garments, ornate capes and 'star of the East' motifs. A popular prop on stage was a water pipe, and Robert Bogdan noted that a Turkish resident in New York was consulted over the initial Circassian Beauty's dress and name. Sideshow postcards emphasised the exotic and erotic qualities of the performers, and studio shots accordingly featured items such as animal skins or palm leaves.

Bogdan (1988)wrote:

> One of the only requirements was that they be physically attractive – by Victorian standards. The "Circassians" were, in fact, indistinguishable from thousands of other nineteenth-century women, and they existed in unlimited supply. All there really was the presentation, a creation that wove the history of science together with tales of erotic intrigue from Asia Minor, current events, and a good portion of showman hype.

Diab (2015) wrote that {spelling in original}:

> The bizarre phenomenon capitalised on the craze created by Johann Friedrich Blumenbach's pseudo-scientific theories of race, which traced the roots of white people to the Caucasus, and his belief that "the purest and most beautiful whites were the Circassians."

These whiter than white circus performers were not actually Circassian and, unlike the ideal of Circassian beauty elsewhere in the West, their hair was not of a luxuriant and smooth silky texture, but was wild and curly, an effect produced through liberal shampooing with beer. They were usually dressed in three-quarter-length-pants and flowing garments, water pipe on stage, telling tales of life in the Turkish harem. Because of the hair style, they became known as the "moss haired girls." (Bogdan 1988).

In 1869 George Washington Morrison Nutt, born in

1848, 29 inches tall, joined Barnum's show. Barnum labeled him *Commander Nutt,* dressed in a Naval Officer's uniform complete with a small dress sword. He toured with Barnum until 1872.

In the 1870s, Captain George Costentenus, born in 1836 partnered with P.T. Barnum. Costentenus became the American Museum's highest grossing act, *The Tattooed Man,* earning more than $1,000 per week {$37,000 per week today}. He claimed that he was a Greek-Albanian prince raised in a Turkish harem and that he had been on a military expedition in Burma when he and three others were captured by "savage natives" and offered a choice: they could either be cut into pieces from toe to head, or receive full-body tattoos and be liberated, hence his number of ornate tattoos, 338 covering his skin except for his nose and the soles of his feet. He later said that his story was made up but was helping him to earn fame and fortune. When he died his will gave half of his fortune to the Greek Church, and half to less fortunate freak show performers (Crockett 2014).

Barnum heard about *The Siberian Dog-Man,* shown in England as "the boy who was raised by wolves in Siberian wilderness." Fedor Adrianovich Jeftichew was born in 1873 with a face covered in hair. Barnum purchased the boy's contract and brought him to the United States in 1884 and renamed him as *Jo-Jo The Dog-Faced Boy,* dressed in a Russian Cavalry uniform. Barnum stated he "had been found in a cave deep in the forests of central Russia, feeding on berries and hunting with a rudimentary club; after enduring a bloody battle to capture the ' "beast," ' hunters taught him to walk upright, wear clothes, and speak like a dignified human." Foder did his part barking and growling and baring his teeth. He was paid $500 a week {$13,00 in today's dollars} (Crockett 2014).

Lucia Zarate, twelve years old from Mexico, joined Barnum's show in 1876. She was twenty inches tall and toured until 1890, when she was stranded on a snowbound train and died of exposure. One of her successors, a diminutive black girl, was billed as *Princess Weenie Wee* (American Heritage 1966).

During the years of his operation, Barnum liked labeling cast members as "Professors": Professor Cromwell; Professors Todd and Stanzrood {accordionists}; Professor McCormick {upside-down walker}; Professor Brunswick {with his statuary}; Professor Smith {seven-octave piano}; Professor Livingston {actor turned phrenologist}; Professor Cosporess {magician}; and Professor Hutchings {the "Lightning Calculator"} (Kunhardt et al 1995).

As the circuses grew in size so did the Freak Shows, all following the same assortment first gathered together by Barnum.

Crockett (2014) noted that:

> By the 1890s, freakshows began to wane in popularity; by 1950, they had nearly vanished.
>
> For one, curiosity and mystery were quelled by advances in medicine: so-called "freaks" were now diagnosed with real, scientifically-explained diagnoses. The shows lost their luster as physical and medical

conditions were no longer touted as miraculous and the fanciful stories told by showmen were increasingly discredited by hard science. As spectators became more aware of the grave nature of the performers' conditions, wonder was replaced by pity.

Movies and television, both of which rose to prominence in the early 20th century, offered other forms of entertainment and quenched society's demand for oddities. People could see wild and astonishing things from the comfort of a theatre or home (by the 1920s), and were less inclined to spend money on live shows. Media also made realities more accessible, further discrediting the stories showmen told: for instance, in a film, audience members could see that the people of Borneo weren't actually as savage as advertised by P.T. Barnum.

But the true death chime of the freakshow was the rise of disability rights. Simply put, taking utter delight in others' physical misfortune was finally frowned upon.

Working Acts.

During the 1890 season, six of the nine sideshow performers were women.

The Girl Shows.
The Elaborate Revue Show
By the 1930's they could be up to 60 people, including a full orchestra, and a singer, in colorful and complex

costumes. Large shows could have up to 200 seats (IISM n.d.)

The Cooch Show.

In the mid-1800's "Posing Shows" featured beautiful ladies posing against painted scenery or historic dioramas often in silhouette behind gossamer curtains in tight stocking that gave the illusion of complete nudity. Cooch dancing was introduced at the 1893 Columbian Exposition in Chicago. It was essentially belly dancing. At that time in the south the term "cooch" referred to female genitals. There were various degrees of nudity, in many times total nudity while "dancing." It was aimed at the adult male audience. In most of the cooch shows there were no seats, the guests just stood around a small stage. There were no comics or novelty acts. One of the jobs was to have someone "watch the back" often patrolling outside the tent to stop men from sneaking inside. One of the bally (outside talker) come-ons (spiel) was: "This show is strictly for gentlemen, You must be over 18 and under 80 to go in this tent. There is a good reason for this rule. If you are under 18 you won't understand it and if you are over 80 you couldn't stand it. This redhot burlesque, carnival hoochie coochie. We guarantee you'll leave our show with your hands in your pockets with a new grip on life" (Reid 2010, ISSM 2013b, Stencell 1999).

Other Tents (Nickell 2005)

[many types having a varying existence]
Illusion Show
Magical illusions, such as the headless girl.
Life Shows
Preserved fetuses in "educational exhibits."

Menageries
> Various animals on display.

Wax Shows
> Wax figures of various notable individuals.

Freak Shows
> Discussed above but often including snake
> charmers as a separate figure.

Other Shows
> Sword swallower, fire eaters, snake charmers,
> and novelty acts, contortion acts, etc.

The Concession Tents.

Pink Lemonade - *Two Stories.*

Henry E. Allott was a famed circus promoter and, later, a feared gambler nicknamed "Bunk Allen." He was so well-known that, when he died in Chicago in 1912, he had obituaries in the New York Times and the Washington Post. According to a 1913 restaurant trade handbook, it was 1872 and Allott was only 14 years old when he had a happy accident. He was in charge of both the candy and lemonade concessions for a circus traveling around the country when he made a life-altering mistake. Either by his own clumsiness or someone else's, he dropped a whole container of red cinnamon candies into a vat of freshly-made lemonade. Within moments, the yellow-hued beverage was stained reddish-pink—a similar color to clown pants (Chetwynd 2012).

This version of the story dates pink lemonade's origins to 1857. In his biography, famed lion tamer George Conklin claims that it was his brother Pete, a legendary clown of the time, who first turned lemonade pink. At the time, Pete worked concessions and was a tumbler with well-known promoter Jerry Mabie's show. One day he was asked to take over as a clown. Pete did and asked for clown's pay. Mabie refused. Pete quit, took his lemonade concession with him and proceeded to follow the circus with two mules, and a covered wagon, selling lemonade. One day he ran out of water. In a panic and with the line of people increasing, he barged into the tent of an old clown friend who was wringing out his red tights into a bucket of water. The cheap dye had left the water pinkish-red. Pete used the water and sold the lemonade as "strawberry-lemonade." Another version is that he took the tub of water in which the bareback rider Fannie Jamieson was soaking her red tights. The ingredients are still: water, tartaric acid, sliced lemon "floaters," and a little red dye. (Jensen 1975, Feiler 2000)..

Cotton Candy.

Candy-makers William Morrison and John C. Wharton of Nashville, Tennessee, invented in 1897 the world's first electric machine that allowed crystallized sugar to be poured onto a heated spinning plate, then pushed by centrifugal force through a series of tiny holes.

They took their product, labeled *Fairy Floss* to the 1904 Louisiana Purchase Exposition (St. Louis World's Fair). It was sold in chipped-wood boxes. They sold 68,655 boxes for 25 cents which was half of the fair admission price. That same fair also introduced the world's first ice-cream cone (Feiler 2000).

Popcorn

Charles Cretors opened a bakery and a confectionery

shop in Decatur, Illinois. He had a steam powered machine to roast peanuts or popcorn in oil. His machine became the first automated machine that could pop popcorn uniformly in its own seasonings.

Charles Cretors took his new popcorn wagon to the Midway of Chicago's Columbian Exposition in 1893 and introduced pop corn to the visitors.

Carmel Corn

Frederick and Louis Rueckheim, two German immigrates open a popcorn store in Chicago and came up with the idea to cover popcorn with molasses to sell in the Midway of Chicago's Columbian Exposition in 1893. They also mixed the "caramel corn" with peanuts. In 1896 they registered that product as "Cracker Jack."

The Corn Dog

The Albert Pick - L. Bart 1929 Wholesale Catalog of Hotel and Restaurant Supplies listed a "Krusty Korn Dog" machine which baked the Korn Dogs inside a corn batter that resembled ears of corn. Carl and Neil Fletcher claimed that they produced "Corny Dog" at the Texas State Fair between 1938-1942. In Springfield, Illinois, the Cozy Dog Drive-In, claimed that they first served corn dogs on a stick 16 June 1946, the same year the Hot Dog On A Stick was served by Dave Barham at Muscle Beach, Santa Monica, California (Funtastic 2017).

Funnel Cake

Batter is swirled around into hot oil using a funnel, creating a lattice of deep-fried dough, served with heaps of powdered sugar, or, cinnamon, chocolate, jelly, and fruit, with around 276 calories per serving. Its origins are the

Pennsylvania Dutch, German immigrants who came to the United States in the 17th and 18th centuries. Around 1879, they developed the baking powder version of a yeast-risen food. The recipe was published in a German cook book of that time as a breakfast or mid-morning treat. The funnel cake was first offered to the public, as a demonstration, at the Kutztown Folk Festival in 1950 (Siciliano-Rosen n. d., FatSecret 2007, GM n. d., KFF n. d.)

☞ Carnivals ☜

Russell and Murray (2004) wrote that:

> The general public's confusing of carnivals and circuses may stem at least in part from the many ways in which the two subcultures have historically been connected: circuses and carnivals have often traveled together (usually for economic reasons), both have often contained sideshows (about which more shortly), and large carnivals have even regularly contained small circuses (though large circuses have never contained small carnivals).

In the circus world the midway is located between the entrance to the big top and the entryway onto the circus grounds. The carnivals were essentially traveling midways (Nickell 2005).

All traveling carnivals have some variety of riding devices, shows or exhibits, concessions, and gaming. In the beginning the carnival was the poor man's entertainment, for the carny it was a supportive family (Miller 2013)

Throughout the 1800s, carnival performers visited rural towns and villages throughout the country. They were usually simple vaudeville, circus, or magic shows. The performers also included modest guessing games without many prizes. (Victor 2017).

In 1902 there were seventeen traveling carnivals in the United States. Soon there were twenty-two touring carnivals playing at street fairs and traveling by railroad. The number grew to forty-six in 1905 and by 1937 there were an estimated 300 carnivals touring the country. In 1969 the number rose to 600 selling over 15 million admission tickets (Doc's Midway Cookhouse 2020b, Nickell 2005).

MacPherson (2008) wrote that:

> "Our fuel costs are four times as much as it was 10 years ago, and we haven't raised our prices in 10 years," said Lon McWhorter, owner of Woonsocket, S.D.-based Mac's Carnival & Attractions, the sole carnival company based in the Dakotas.

> About 345 carnival companies travel the U.S. each year, down from about 400 a decade ago. Many are family-owned businesses, and they need to be assured of big attendance to come to a fair.

Carousels

Benjamin and Williams (2016) wrote that:

> The makers were the pioneers, those innovative and brave enough to venture into unchartered waters with their simple machines and primitive animals. From humble

beginnings of going around in circles, the earliest carousels set the stage for what was to follow – much larger and more elaborate, animated, illuminated carousels that glitter and dazzle.

Initially carousels were permanent installations that rotated with horses or non-horse structures to ride upon, none of which rode up and down.

The carousel industry began to develop in the late 19th century by immigrants such as: Gustav Dentzel from Germany; and, Charles W.F. Dare from England.

Dentzel made carousels from 1867 to 1928. The Philadelphia Toboggan Company, incorporated 1904, built: carousels; wooden roller coasters; and, a roller coaster car, called "toboggans." It bought the Dentzel company in 1928, known for their elaborate carvings and decorations on carousels, 1904 - 1934.

Dare apparently started as a toy manufacturer, in the late 1850's, but eventually formed the *New York Carousel M.F.G. Company* that existed from 1889 until 1898. The company manufactured three kinds of carousels: a swinging carousel with no platform, which was essentially a peaked, circular tent that rotated above bare ground with suspended, hanging horses; a carousel with a swinging platform with stationary animals; and, a galloping horse carousel with horses in a jumping pose on rockers. The early manufacturers set the style for the horses for all the later manufacturers. This style had apparently had been modeled after the early "hobby horse" on rockers ca. 1880's (Benjamin and Williams

2016).

C. W. Parker, of Abilene, Kansas, bought in 1892 and began to produce the Armitage/Herschell track machine. In 1894 he started the *Parker Carnival Supply Company*. In 1896 it became the *C. W. Parker Amusement Company* also building shooting galleries, Ferris wheels, and other equipment. By 1905 he had four full-sized carousels in carnivals. He relocated to Leavenworth, Kansas, and built a new factory in 1911 which built hundreds of small touring carousels. He died in 1932. The company, run by his son, endured until 1955 (LHMA n.d., DCHS 2011).

Allan Herschell and James Armitage, a trained Scottish machinist, created the *Armitage Herschell Company* in 1873, in North Tonawanda, New York, initially manufacturing steam boilers. The company began to make hand-carved carousels animals in 1883, specializing in rigid posed horse and portable machines, packed for easy shipping. This specializing led to a 50 percent expansion of their business. They made, 1915 to 1959, 3,000 portable carousels. In 1960, the *Chance Manufacturing Company*, in Witchita, Kansas, bought the business and moved it to Kansas (IISM 2015, TOM 2013).

Portable Ferris Wheel

Today "Ferris wheels that are designed to be transported on the road from one location to another must conform to the overall width, height, and length restrictions for highway vehicles. Although these restrictions vary from state to state, most states limit the trailer width to 8.5 ft (2.6 m), the height to 13.5 ft (4.1 m), and the length to 55 ft (16.8

m). No matter how big or small the ferris wheel is when it is opened and in operation, it must fold down to meet these restrictions when it is traveling on the highway" (Made How 2020).

C. W. F. Dare's company made the *Dare Aerial Swing*, in 1870. It was portable with wooden Ferris wheels in either 20-foot or 30-foot diameters (Gale 2017, Anderson 1992).

The Strobel Company, in Marion, Ohio began manufacturing in 1885, the "Rotable Pleasure Wheel," a 25-foot diameter wheel with eight seats rotated by a light steel cable running through a grove on the rim of the wheel using a small gasoline engine. It was, perhaps, a co-design of Frederick Strobel and Edward Huber, Marion's best known inventor. It was one of the earliest mass-produced portable wheels which could be hauled by one wagon in one load (Anderson 1992).

The Conderman Brothers of Indiana made a 35-foot portable Ferris wheel in 1899. It was made of metal pipes and carried 10 double seats, two adults to a seat. They also made an electric car in 1898 (Pursell 2015, Made How 2020, Poole 2011).

William E. Sullivan, a bridge builder and inventor, designed a cable-driven 45-foot diameter wheel with 12 three-passenger seats. With James H. Clements, machinist, he built their first wheel on 23 March 1900. He created the *Eli Bridge Company* in 1906 in Roodhouse, Illinois, and started production. He moved his business's permanent home to Jacksonville, Illinois and today makes a 12-seat and a 6-seat mobile Ferris wheel. The company had always been a family affair with Lee A. Sullivan, Jr., becoming the manager in 1966

(How Made 2020, Anderson 1992).

Tilt-A-Whirl

Herbert Sellner made the first one in 1926. It had nine cars, holding 2 passengers each. When it appeared at the 1926 Minnesota State Fair. In 7 days it had 4,233 riders. He opened a factory in Faribault, Minnesota, 1927. The design was modified in 1928 and took 3 men to operate: the clutch operator, the ticket taker, and the ticket seller. It had 9 cars, 3 each of red, orange, and blue, holding a total of 36 riders. Its movements were described as: tilting, sweeping, spinning, sliding, skidding, rounding, rotating, rising, revolving, hesitating, flying, falling, curving, and circling. Sellner died in 1930 with his company being mostly run by his wife and other Sellner relatives. In 2011 the company was sold to Larson International, Inc., in Plainview, Texas (MNOPEDIA 2019).

Swing Ride

It is often called a Swing Carousel as it utilizes the same action but replaces the carousel animals, etc., with swings suspended by chains. Henry Guy Traver, trained machinist and mechanical engineer, patented the design in 1904, naming it the *Traver Circle Swing*. It simulated the experience of flying which was of great interest at that time. The cars, baskets, or boats would spin 20-25 feet from the ground. The company went bankrupt in 1907. A number of other companies began making the ride afterwards (HC 2020, Oswald 2019)

Zipper

The overall general design from 1968, was based on an earlier ride called The Swooper. The Swooper was invented in 1928 by Sellner Manufacturing. The new design had the Zipper's frame rotate as the cars travel around the arm. Chance Manufacturing, Chance Industries, Inc., manufactured 222 units over the past half century, 1968 - 2001. *Popular Mechanics* suggested the ride was "one of the strangest rides in the world" (Shaw 2019).

Scrambler

Richard Harris built the first one and set it up in 1938 at the Lakewood Fairgrounds in Lakewood Heights, Atlanta, Georgia. He received a patent for the design in 1941. *The Eli Bridge Company* rode-tested it in 1953 and sold five in 1954/1955. It had 3 arms with 12 cars, holding 24-adults, or, 36 children, with the arms rotating clockwise at 9-12 revolutions per minute while the cars also rotated. They have sold around 490 units (Coaster Guy 2012, Wiki 2020).

Carnival Shows

It has been suggested that Frank Charles Bostock, of Darlington, England, and his partners, the Ferari brothers, Francis and Joseph, were the beginnings of the touring carnival business in America for two years, 1893-1894, as the *Bostock-Ferari Midway Carnival Co.* In 1893 Bostock and his wife, Susannah Ethel Bailey, lived in 1 wagon and had 2 wagons that housed 4 monkeys, 5 parrots, 3 lions, 1 sheep, and 1 boxing kangaroo (who wore regulation boxing gloves).

It has been suggested that their show structure became the nucleus around which many of the early street-fair showmen built their midways. On 27 October 1893, one of the lions, named Wallace, escaped from his cage in a 12x20 stable at the Portman Hotel, 129 18th Street, and attacked and killed a horse. Around ten-o-clock in the morning, R.F. "Tody" Hamilton with his helpers, Felix McDonald and George Conklin, from the Barnum & Bailey Circus, arrived with pulley blocks, ropes, and hooks. By 4 p.m. they finally had the lion back in his cage. Bostock returned to England (US n.d., THC 2013).

Reithoffer Shows

Julius Reithoffer emigrated from Germany in the mid-1880s and opened a general store in Duryea, Pennsylvania. In 1896 he bought a stream driven carousel and soon thereafter he bought a Ferris wheel. He sold his store and invested in his show, The *Mighty Reithoffer Shows*. The family took to the road on the East Coast in the summer. When the Packard Company began to produce the world's first large trucks they hauled their equipment that way. He invented rides including the first automobile kiddie ride. After WWI Patrick Edward Reithoffer, Jr. bought new trucks and put diesel generators inside semi-trucks to provide electricity to run their rides. They build *housetrucks*, the first motorhomes to house the carnival people. They moved their winter quarters to Gibsonton, Florida and started buying rides with large capacity in the 1960's. Pat created a centralized ticket system, the first in the industry. In the 1970s, Pat's son, Pat III and Rick took over management. With expansion in the equipment, they created and managed the Blue (Rick) and Orange (Pat III) Units. In 1983 they added the Dutch wheel, a portable big wheel. Led lighting was added in 2006. Today they play 40 fairs a year with 100 rides (Reithoffer 2020, IISM 2013).

Canton Carnival Company

Frank W. Gaskill, an Alliance, Ohio, hotel owner, started his operation on 30 May 1899. The Order of Elks (Akron, Canton, Zanesville) formed a committee to start a carnival that would bring money into local towns. Gaskill had a contracting agent develop a route and two men to assemble the midway as well as an advance man to assemble local labor and materials, erecting banner frames, loading the canvas and other materials on the railroad cars, and began touring to other towns (Nickell 2005, Stencell 1999).

Wade Shows

Based in Livonia, Michigan, and founded as the *Imperial Shows*, by Leander "Lee" Wade in 1912. After he retired it was renamed, *Joyland Midway Attractions*. His son, G. W. Wade in 1916 started the *W. G. Wade Shows*, touring throughout Michigan. His son Wallace G. "Glenn" Wade operated his own midway company and then merged it with the *W. G. Wade Shows*. Then Frank Zaishik bought the *W. G. Wade Shows*, including the 100 amusement rides and attractions. They have offices in Michigan and Florida, providing midways to state fairs in a number of states: New York, Alabama, North Carolina, Oklahoma, Missouri, Delaware, and Nebraska (Wiki 2015).

Royal American Shows

Carl J. Sedlmay and his partner bought the *Seigrist & Silbon Shows* in 1921. Sedlmay bought out his partner and changed the name to *Royal American Shows* in 1923. The show was headquartered in Tampa, Florida. As he traveled in both Canada and the United States, he used the term *Royal* for Canada and *American* for the U.S. It was considered to be one of the largest carnivals in America. By 1967 the show had over 800 people and traveled on 80+ railroad cars hauling livestock, equipment, carpenters, canvas men, electricians, painters, full working machine shops with mills, lathes, and drills, welders, mechanics, cookhouse, portable showers, and a mail department. He died in 1965. His son and grandson, Carl J. Sedlmayr, Jr., and Carl J. Sedlmayr III began handling the show. The last show was in Lubbock, Texas, in October 1977. The Royal American Shows were sold by Norton Auctioneers of Coldwater, Michigan. Carnival executives, employees, railroad and circus buffs from 26 states, and two countries, attended the sale at the winter headquarters (IISM 2020, USM 1924).

Strates Shows

James E. Strates, immigrated from Greece in 1909, worked as an athletic show wrestler, and bought *Southern Tier Shows* in 1923, renaming it *James E. Strates Shows* in 1932. The show consisted of 15 concessions, 3 sideshows, a merry-go-round, Ferris wheel, and 5 hard-rubber tire trucks. In 1934 he bought 5 flatbed railroad cars and 17 trucks to haul the show's equipment which expanded in 1938 to 25 railroad cars and 61 trucks and wagons. In the winter they stored everything in a barn in Mullins, South Carolina. It burned down on 22 December 1945, with the exception of the train. The show was rebuilt and expanded to 20 sideshows, 21 rides, and surplus anti-aircraft searchlights in 1946. By 1953 the show was the fourth largest in the nation with 300 employees. The winter quarters were relocated from the Deland, Florida, fairground to Taft next to Orlando, Florida. He built and managed the show until his death in 1959, when his son, E. James Strates, assumed responsibility. It has a seven-month season with 400 employees and families operating many of the games, concessions, and games. The show travels with 61 rail cars and 34 trucks (Strates Shows, Inc. n.d.)

Stipe Shows

Lance and Mame Stipe started, in the Great Depression era of the mid-1930s, a part-time business at local fairs and festivals, selling popcorn and root beer. In 1948, Lance bought a Ferris wheel, a merry-go-round, and several kiddie rides and toured *Stipe Shows* in eastern Minnesota and western Wisconsin. Mame died in 1975 with children Bill and Mary taking over the business. Their father died in 1978. Bill died in 1992 with his son Barry becoming General Manager. Mary died in 2007. Barry's son Kyle now manages operations and daily activity. The carnival moves 15 rides, other vehicles, and about 15 people, throughout eastern Minnesota and western Michigan (SS 2020).

Crafts 20 Big Show

The show was started in 1933 by Roger and Frank

Warren and their step-father, Orville Neil Craft. In 1937 they were: *Craft's Exposition; Craft's Imperial; 20 Big Show*. By 1947 they had 42 rides, 12 shows, 111 concessions, 6 searchlights, and 38 neon light towers. At the death of Orville in 1960, his wife sold: the North Hollywood winter quarters, which was more valuable than the shows; the majority of the equipment, most of which had become worn and could not meet California inspection standards, some to Bobby Cohn's West Coast Shows who used the salvageable equipment for his operation, some Pete Sutton of the *Great Sutton Shows*, and some sold as scrap to Mexico (Doc's Midway Cookhouse 2015).

Jolly Shows

Frank Joseph bought in 1939 his first amusement ride, an Eyerly Aircraft, "Roll-o-Plane." Later he bought an "Octopus" and "Spitfire." It operated seasonally at local amusement parks, church bazaars, firemen's carnivals, and county fairs throughout Maryland through the late 1940's. His oldest son, Pete, began to help with the business in this late teens. They partnered in 1958 with Bill Enfante, another small carnival operator, from Washington, D.C. and formed *Jolly Shows*. They operated within the Washington, D.C. metropolitan area in the 1960s and early 1970s. In 1973 Infante died and they purchased his interest in the business, incorporating as *Frank Joseph & Sons*. The carnival, operated by grandsons Randy, Peter, and Paul, operates exclusively in Maryland and Northern Virginia (Jolly Shows 2020).

Gopher State Expositions

Arthur and Mildred Forcier started a carnival, *Gopher State Shows*, based in Saint Cloud, Minnesota in 1948 and was operated by the parents and their eight children. Two of the children, Arthur Jr., and Shirley, bought the show in 1968 changing the name in 1981 to *Gopher State Expositions*. As of 2020, their children, Randy and Tony Forcier, operate in Minnesota and Iowa from May-October, with 25-30 rides, and 20-30 concessions (GSE 2020).

Golden Wheel Amusements

Claire Morton and her husband came to Alaska with her husband to pick up a piece of carnival equipment, an Octopus ride, from the local carnival operator who had gone bankrupt in 1976. The organizers of *Fur Rondy*, Fur Rendezvous, the self-styled "largest winter festival in North America," in Anchorage, Alaska, begged the couple to stay and put on that year's show. They agreed and began to operate the only carnival in Alaska. Clare Morton died, 18 December 2018. Jacqueline Leavitt, one of her daughters, owned the company. Since 1910 *The Legacy Group*, Chugiak, Alaska, was doing business as *Golden Wheel Amusements* (Wohlforth 2019).

Campy's Amusements

Rocco Campanell established *Campy's Amusements* in 1969. His son, Robert, took over in 1972 with Robert's wife, Ann in charge of operations. As of 2020 their children, Keith and Karyn, and Karyn's husband, Paul, run the carnival of 20 rides and 16 games, from April to the third week of October, throughout New Jersey (Campy's 2020).

Brown's Amusements

Danny and Sherry Brown, second generation amusement industry people, and independent concession owners, in 1979 expanded into *Brown's Amusements* and grew to 12 rides, 10 games and 1 food concession (1996). Their route runs through Colorado, Wyoming, Idaho, Arizona, Utah, and New Mexico. As of 2020 they now own and operate over 50 pieces of equipment and added, in 2019, a *Jumping Jumbos Elephant* ride and 3 new food wagons. They have two units with winter quarters in Phoenix, Arizona. They haul around 35 carnival rides in owned 42 DOT-qualified trailers and box trucks, following the same regulations as any independent trucker or freight carrier drivers with commercial driver's licenses and keep distances, between carnival locations to under 150 miles (Brown's Amusements 2020, Carnival Warehouse 2019, Gallagher 2019).

Frazier Shows

In 1982 Cecil Frazier started and incorporated *Frazier Shows of America*. He sold it to Steve (Corporation President, former concession manager) and Julie (third generation carnival owner) Broetsky in 2001/2002. The carnival had 16 rides. In 2018 the carnival had 30 rides with only 4 of the previous 16 being retained. The carnival travels through Arizona, New Mexico, Texas, Colorado, and Nebraska (Frazier Shows 2020, Davis 2018b).

Fantasy Amusement Company

Bill Johnson, during the ages 11-14, started picking up the balls at the "Milk Bottle Game" for the owner, Bill Knight. He began, at age 18, to run a unit for Knight. He bought a ride, *The Swinger,* at age 24, and became a Ride Supervisor for *Loop Amusement* the next year. When he was 26 he bought 2 rides, managed 7 games, and started *Fantasy Amusement Company, Inc.,* of Prospect Heights, Illinois. Soon he and his wife, Mary, had 8 rides, a few games, and a popcorn wagon. Today they have over 40 rides, games, and concession, serving the greater Chicagoland area, Central and Northern Illinois, and Northwest Indiana. Many of their children, and the children's spouses work in various occupations in the operation during the May-September season (FAC 2012).

Great Northern Carnival

Vern (Swede) and Rene Mattfeld, and their son and daughter, started *A Great Northern A'Fair* in 1996 with a Ferris wheel and a couple of food wagons, serving southwestern Arizona, northern New Mexico, and southern Colorado. In 1988, they acquired *Mountainland Amusement Company* in Salt Lake City and moved it to Arizona. The carnival, considered mid-sized, had 18 rides, 10-15 games, and many food wagons. It was renamed *Big Sky Amusements.* They tried to cut back their route because trucking was a major issue. The carnival was a family operation until 1997. Their sons, Steve (*Sun Valley Rides*) and Tim (*A Great Northern A'Fair*) operate the two carnivals as of 2020. The operation carries a base unit of 10-12 rides, 8-10 game concessions, and 1-3 food concessions

(Greatnotherncarnival 2019, Davis 2018a, SVR 2020).

Coleman Brothers Shows

In 1916, Richard "Dick" Colman bought for $250 a steam-powered merry go round that was under the Portland Bridge and ran it on the St. John Church property. The Portland Bridge is a historic suspension bridge in New Portland, Maine. It was built in the mid-19th century, one of four 19th-century suspension bridges in Maine. His purchase was the beginning of his carnival show. He died in 2017 and his children ,Mary Oaks and Tim Coleman, have run the show each summer with 22 rides, 7 food stands, 15 games, with about 25 stops in Connecticut, New York, and Massachusetts. The winter headquarters are in barns built by the students of Vinal Technical High School in Middleton, Connecticut (Beals 2016, Day 2019).

James H. Drew Exposition

Jimmy and Evangeline Drew started in 1948 with a Ferris wheel and merry-go-round and always featured an antique organ. Several times a year they put up the *Space Wheel*, manufactured in 1958 by the Valare Brothers, all rotating parts made by Douglas Aircraft for the Seattle World's Fair. The family runs a single unit of 30 rides (up to 60 if needed) from their home in Augusta, Georgia. They were a food concessions operation with a few games but became primarily ride oriented. They operate from March to mid-November in central Georgia, the Carolinas, West Virginia, Kentucky, and Indiana (Powell 2019, Davis 2020). Drew (Davis 2020) noted that:

> ... old standbys such as cotton candy, candy apples, corn dogs and
> funnel cakes as crowd favorites.

> When you get North of the Ohio River, funnel cakes don't sell; it's
> elephant ears that sell. Different kinds of candy apples sell in
> different towns. In the smaller towns in Georgia, it's plain red
> candy apples. In more urban markets, it's apples with nuts that do
> the best. And north of the Ohio, it's caramel apples. And if you
> get within 50 miles of the Canadian border, donuts sell a lot. Get
> away from the border, and they just do not sell.

Nonweiler Amusements

William T. and Olivia Shea Nonweiler journeyed from Pennsylvania to Georgia in 1951, in their living quarters of a converted bakery truck, selling popcorn. They started Nonweiler Amusements in 1950 with the popcorn machine, a Ferris wheel, and a merry-go-round, building their own concession stands and renting them to others. By 2019 they had 16 rides, games, and concessions, operating only in Pennsylvania, from their hometown, Lehighton (Endy 2009, Nonweiler n.d.).

Tons Of Fun Shows

Otto Pfeffer started *Otto's Amusements, Inc.*, in 1957 in Pottsville, Pennsylvania, with a homemade ride constructed from a P-51 Mustang external fuel tank. He eventually bought rides ranging from a pony ride to merry-go-round. Warren Imes booked games on *Otto's Amusements, Inc., Penn Valley Shows, Oscars Amusements*, and *S & S Amusements*. In 1977, Warren and Betty Imes started D & S Concessions with 7 concessions. They bought *Oscar's Amusements* in 1979. Their daughter Suellen married David Pfeffer and formed *Tons Of*

Fun Shows in 1991 with their concessions and 3 rides. By 1996 they had 8 rides and 10 games. Their operation grew to 23 rides in 2018 (TFS n.d., Freese 2018).

A Short Note: I started looking at every website from a list of 205 carnivals (which seems to be a pretty good sample). Most of them have some sort "About Us" comment stating that they and their family have long term connections to the carnival world. Of these 205, sufficient data could only be found to write these small histories of 19 carnivals.

☞ The Wild West Shows ☜

McMurty (2005) wrote that:

> Buffalo Bill and Annie Oakley were, in my opinion, the first American superstars – in 1880 and 1890's, at the height of their fame, their images were recognized the world over.

> He was the hero of no less than seventeen hundred dime novels, many of them written by the wildly prolific pulper Colonel Prentiss Ingraham.

I would suggest that P. T. Barnum was probably the first, although for somewhat different reasons.

It has been suggested that the romantic image of The West began with many of the expeditions traveling into the west that brought along artists to document what they found and saw. This art tended to be a combination of romantic landscapes and "pretensions to scientific accuracy" as William H. Goetzmann and William N. Goetzmann wrote (2009). They also stated that much of the art tended to create the West as they knew it ought to have looked, arguing that romanticized visions of the West were far more relevant than scientific ones buried in federal archives. These images of the sublime helped to create "a series of sacred places across the continent" and were the essential founding documents of the national parks. The grey area between science and art provided just enough room for embellishment, a skill that would prove increasingly pivotal to the creation of "The West" that was to become the Buffalo Bill show.

There were dime novels, short prose novelettes, about distant, romantic figures, the mountain men by the 1840s (McMurtry 2005).

Buffalo Bill's Wild West Shows (1883-1916).

In 1846 William Frederick Cody was born (February 26) in Scott County, Iowa. Iowa became a state on December 28 in the same year.

His father, Isaac Cody was born 15 September 1811 in Toronto, Canada. In 1834 he married Martha Miranda O'Connor. She died in 1835 following the birth of a daughter, Martha. He went to Cincinnati to study medicine but decided to move to the territory of Iowa to farm near LeClaire, Iowa. He wed, in 1840, Mary Ann Bonsell Laycock, of Cincinnati. They had seven children: Samuel, Julia, William F., Eliza, Helen, May and Charles.

In 1852 Isaac moved his family from their home near Le Clair, Iowa, on the Walnut Grove, further west of Le Claire to a large farm.

The territories of Nebraska and Kansas were opened to settlement claims and Issac staked his claim in the Salt Creek Valley, Kansas, right where the Salt Creek Trail passed by. He helped found the town of Grasshopper Falls (renamed later as Valley Falls.) The slavery debate between Kansas and Missouri resulted in a border war that ran from 1854 until

1861. He operated a trading post near the Kickapoo Indian Agency. He made many speeches in favor of the admission of Kansas into the Union. By the end of summer they lived in a seven-room log home. In 1855 he was stabbed in the back {Warren (2005) states "in the side"} by a proslavery Missourian, Charles Dunn, in Leavenworth County and was forced to leave the territory, for his life was constantly in danger. Dunn was arrested but did not lose his job with Elijah Cody, Isaac's brother. In 1856, Issac was one of the builders of a mill in Grasshopper Falls and was elected to the freestate legislature in the same year. He died in 1857, following an April outbreak of scarlet fever and measles from a nearby settler's camp (World Press 2018, Sachse 2011, Cody Archive n.d., McMurtry 2005, Fleming 2016, Warren 2005).

William F. Cody often related killing his first Indian who helped attack during a cattle drive in 1857 near the South Platte River. There are numerous versions of what actually happened without any clear and accepted version. It became a creation myth of the legend that would be circulated and then be promoted by Cody (McMurty 2005).

William Russell created in 1859, the *Leavenworth and Pike's Peak Express*. The route would run from Leavenworth to Denver along the Smoke Hill River in western Kansas, with 26 stage stations. Cody worked as an ox-team wagon driver hauling hay to Leavenworth (Warren 2005, Johnson 1953).

The city of Denver, population of 4,759, induced the *Leavenworth and Pike's Peak Express Company* to open an office in return for fifty-three town lots and shares in the town company. The stage carried passengers, freight, and mail into the settlement and took passengers, mail, and gold out.

Denver City gained prominence as the hub of commerce and finance (Simmons and Simmons 2016).

Bill Cody at the age of eleven, began to work as a mounted messenger for Majors and Russell, a freighting and transport firm, headquartered in Leavenworth, supplying Colorado and Utah military posts. Leavenworth, the biggest trail town, was founded in 1854 on the Platte River road to California, lying at the junction of the Missouri River and the various routes west. Cody delivered messages on mule back for 3 miles each way traveling from the headquarters to the telegraph office at Ford Leavenworth. In the 1850s and 1860s it was normal for youth to do a man's work at the age of eleven or twelve. Later he would become a drover, cowboy, herdsman, and teamster (McMurtry 2005, Fleming 2016, Warren 2005).

Cody met James Butler "Wild Bill" Hickok (nearly ten years old that Cody) when Hickok and he worked for the stagecoach and wagon-freighting company. They remained friends until Hickok's murder in Deadwood, South Dakota, 2 August 1876.

Russell, Majors, and Waddell started the Pony Express runs in April 1860, from St. Joseph, Missouri to Sacramento, California. There were 190 stations, five hundred horses, and about eighty riders. At that time it took almost a month to deliver mail to California by boat. John Butterfield ran a similar system that nearly touched the Mexican border and ended in San Diego, California. The first rider out of St. Joseph was Bob Haslam. Cody's claim for extreme distances many have been inflated for dramatic purposes. By November 1860 the telegraph had linked the east and west coast. Cody's job with the Pony Express required him to ride farther and faster that normal but he was in the central plains, a place he came to over and over, working mostly alone. The Pony Express job was grueling for horse and man. Few of the eighty riders lasted for the eighteen months than the service existed. He quit in 1861. The veracity of Cody's Pony Express rider days as one writer stated was "real, if possibly exaggerated" (McMurty 2005, Fleming 2016).

During the American Civil War (1861–65), Cody first served as a Union scout in campaigns against the Kiowa and Comanche and in 1863 (some accounts state February 1864) enlisted with the Seventh Kansas Cavalry which was organized and mustered into services on 27 April 1863, in Davenport, Kansas. The unit saw action in Missouri and Tennessee. Cody mustered out as a private after 18 months. The unit was mustered out on 22 June 1866 in Sioux City, Kansas (IPC 1882, McMurty 2005).

In 1866 Cody married Louisa Frederici. He turned the Cody homestead into a hotel, the *Golden Rule House*. Six months later he headed west. His wife returned to her parent's house in St. Louis (Fleming 2016).

The Railroad Act of 1862 stated: *An Act to aid in the construction of a railroad and telegraph line from the Missouri river to the Pacific ocean, and to secure to the government the use of the same for postal, military, and other purposes.*

The Kansas Pacific Railway advertised in October 1857, for a buffalo hunter as their track had moving into the great plains and the twelve hundred workers needed to be fed. Tanneries paid as much as $3.00 per hide and 25¢ for each tongue. Among the many hunters were Wyatt Earp, Bat

Masterson, Pat Garrett, Wild Bill Hickok, and William F. Cody (Legends of America 2020a, Fleming 2016).

Cody made his living as a contract buffalo hunter for the Goddard Brothers, October 1857 - May 1868, feeding the crews laying track across Kansas for the Kansas Pacific Railroad. He was paid $500 a month for 12 buffalo a day. A number of the hunters and others had nicknames that were a variation of "Buffalo Bill:" Charles "Buffalo" Jones; William J. "Buffalo Bill" Wilson; "Buffalo Billy" Brooks; William C. Tomlins "Buffalo Bill of the Black Hills;" William Comstock, sometimes called "Buffalo Bill,"and William F. "Buffalo Bill" Cody. Cody also hunted buffalo to provide meat to feed the soldiers at Fort Wallace.

Newspapers reported in December 1967 that Hickok had come to stay in Hays City, Kansas. As a Deputy U.S. Marshal, on 28 March 1868, he picked up eleven Union Army deserters, charged with stealing government property. Hickok, assigned to bring the men to Topeka for trial, requested a military escort from Fort Hays. He was assigned William F. Cody, and one sergeant, and five privates.

To determine who would be the real "Buffalo Bill" a wager was made and a contest was staged west of Oakley in Logan County, Kansas in 1867. The contest was to see which hunter could harvest the most buffalo in one day. William F. Cody won the contest 69 to 46. There are various forms of this story varying from "it is true" to "it was made up" (McMurty 2005, Fleming 2016, Coppock 2015). Either way the "legend of Buffalo Bill Cody" became alive and well.

The Indian Removal Act (1830) forced 46,000 Indians to move from the east of America to the west. It was a place that President Jackson declared as *Indian Territory*, protected from existing Indians and white settlers.

The Indian Trade and Intercourse Act (1834) created a *permanent* Indian Frontier of all land west of the Mississippi River, not including Louisiana or Arkansas, with White settlers banned from settling on Indian Territory or selling guns or alcohol to the Indians. This region was protected by the US Army with forts and military roads.

During the California gold rush in 1848, people followed the roads from east to west over the Closed territory.

In 1850 the government pressed the Indians to cede their lands, using economic sanctions, military strength, and treaties.

Cody's abilities as a scout had him involved in the 1869-1870 prairie campaigns of military activities which were largely futile (McMurty 2005).

He met the then Colonel Judson (also known as Ned Buntline) at Fort McPherson who accompanied Cody on a Fifth Calvary Expedition to Fort Sedgwick, Colorado, with Cody relating his past adventures. It is also claimed that in 1869 Cody and Buntline became friends after the two met on a train from California to Nebraska (Fleming 2016, McMurty 2005).

After the American Civil War, stories and inexpensive dime novels depicting the American West and frontier life were becoming common. Some of the early authors were Ned Buntline (the pen name of Edward Zane Carroll Judson, Sr.) and Prentiss Ingraham. Buntline claimed that the nickname for the hero of his serial novel *Buffalo Bill, the King of the Border Men,* published in the *New York Weekly* beginning 23 December 1869, was his creation. While it was claimed as the "wildest and truest story," if was pure fiction. In December 1872, Buntline turned his novel into a theatrical production. *The Scouts of the Prairie* debuted in Chicago, featuring Buntline, Cody, Texas Jack Omohundro, and the Italian-born ballerina Giuseppina Morlacchi. The show toured the American theater circuit for two years (McMurty 2005, Fleming 2016).

This was probably the beginning of Cody's enhancement of the Buffalo Bill mythology as typified by the later publication of his tales (Cody 1917).

Texas Jack, Jr. was the adopted boy found by his father, shortly after the Civil War, when he and his sisters were orphaned by an Indian attack. He adopted the name of his father, Texas Jack Omohundro. He worked as a scout much the same as Cody and joined him in Buntline's stage production. He became a sharpshooter and trick rider in shows. In 1902, Will Rogers asked Jack for a job wrangling the tents or the horses, but was asked if he could do a rope trick. He did and was hired.

Early in 1870 Cody guided wealthy men out onto the prairie to hunt as an economic activity.

On 15 June 1876, Lieutenant Colonel George Armstrong Custer arrived with six, or, seven hundred, men to attack an Indian encampment on the Little Bighorn stream. He with a small force of men ran head long into two thousand warriors. 268 soldiers died, including Custer, and 55 were severely wounded,

Cody spent years guiding, then trying his hand at

cattle raising, with about 4,500 cattle on 4,000 acres of land. On the 4ᵗʰ of July 1882, he held a cowboy contest, the *Old Glory Blow Out*, in North Platte, Nebraska. He had hoped to attract at least one hundred people to enter the contest. He got almost 1,000. The contest grew into the rodeo shows that rapidly became a permanent fixture today in many places in the United States (McMurty 2005, Fleming 2016).

In May 1883, Cody and W. F. "Doc" Carver opened the *Wild West, Rocky Mount and Prairie Exhibition* in Omaha, Nebraska. The original title was much longer: *The Wild West, W. F. Cody and W. F. Carver's Rocky Mountain and Prairie Exhibition*. Cody wanted to have recreated scenes, melodramas (like Custer's Last Stand), even if they were, in many cases stretches of imagination of western history, as well as sharpshooters, trick horse riders, etc. Carver had much the same past experiences as Cody. He was a teamster, did some scouting, fought in several skirmishes with Indians, and shot buffalo (McMurty 2005, Fleming 2016).

Indian actors, mostly Plains Nations, such as the Lakota, were hired to participate in *Indian Races*, alleged historic battles, and noisy scenes attacking whites, portraying *exotic savages*, the then popular image of savagery and wildness in the *Wild West*.

McMurtry (2005) wrote that:

> Somehow Cody succeeded in taking a very few
> elements of Western life – Indians, buffalo,
> stagecoach, and his own superbly mounted self
> – and creating an illusion that successfully

stood for a reality that had been almost wholly different.

It was, in his mind, and in the minds of most of the spectators, history, not fiction – easy to understand fiction that allowed the audience to participate vicariously in the great and glorious adventure that had been the settling of the West, and enterprise not yet wholly concluded even in 1886.

Prior to the establishment of Cody's show the endurance shoot was a popular form of entertainment. The shooters fired thousands of bullets at various targets, including pigeons. The pigeon shoots gave the language the term "stool pigeon," which was the term for the pigeon tethered to lure the other pigeons into range of the shooters. By the time Cody opened his first show the shooters were mainly shooting at wooden blocks, glass balls, and clay pigeons. George Ligowsky of Cincinnati invented the first clay target in 1880 to replace the glass balls. The traps cost $20 and a thousand targets were $20 (McMurty 2005, THF 2020, RJD 1951).

Cody worked on reorganizing his show in 1884 to make it new and took it to Chicago, New York, and New Orleans. Their steamboat collided with another paddle wheeler near Rodney Landing, Mississippi, losing wagons, camp equipment, scenery, costumes and props, but saving most of the horses, and the Deadwood stagecoach. It rained for forty-four days. The show lost sixty thousand dollars.

In 1885 Annie Oakley joined the show and was named

The Peerless Wing and Rifle Shot.

Phoebe Ann (Annie) Mosey was born 13 August 1860, the sixth child of nine of which seven survived, in a log cabin less than two miles northwest of Woodland, now Willowdell, in Darke County, Ohio, a rural county along the state's border with Indiana. Her parents, Susan Wise, age 18, and Jacob Mosey, age 49, married in 1848. They were Quakers of English descent from Hollidaysburg, Blair County, Pennsylvania. There is a stone-mounted plaque in the vicinity of the site, which was placed by the Annie. They had previously lived in a rented and then purchased farm in Patterson Township, Darke County, Ohio, around 1855. Her father died in 1866. Annie and her sister, Sarah Ellen, were put into the Darke County Infirmary, the county poor farm. There Annie learned to sew and decorate. In the spring of 1870 she was given to a couple who held her in near slavery. She ran away in 1872, back to her home, and began to trap and hunt local game which she sold to local shopkeepers, Samson and Katzenberger in Greenville, Ohio, who in turn sold it to hotels. Annie did both. The grocers liked her so much that they gave her a new shotgun, a Parker sixteen-gauge, one of the best made along with a container of high-grade gunpowder. Her income helped support her family. In Cincinnati, on Thanksgiving Day a traveling show marksman, Frank E. Butler, an Irish immigrant, bet per side (the equivalent to $2,328 in 2019) with Jack Frost, a Cincinnati hotel owner, that he could beat any local shooter. Frost arranged a shooting match between Butler and the 15-year-old Annie, then five feet tall and weighing around one hundred pounds, dressed moderately. Butler lost the match and the bet. Butler began courting Annie and they married a year later. The shooting match is often dated as 1875, other accounts suggest that it was 1881. As Annie and her husband began performing together she adopted Annie Oakley as her stage name. They joined Buffalo Bill's show in 1885 {some accounts state 1886}. The show played at Queen Victoria's Golden Jubilee in 1887 and was staged throughout Europe. When the show was touring Europe, Charles Lancaster, an English gunsmith made a light twelve-gauge shotgun, weighing six pounds, for Annie. Later Annie and her husband left the show and then returned in 1889. She earned more than any other performer in the show, $100 a week, except for Cody (McMurty 2005, Fleming 2016).

In June of 1886 Cody located his show for the summer on Staten Island, advertising it as *America's National Entertainment*. Adjacent to the show grounds there was an encampment, including a tipi village with other personnel housed in tents, log cabins, and adobe huts, and a stable for 800 animals. Visitors were encouraged to wander freely and even visit when Cody's personal tent was open. The total area was about two city blocks with 140 tents, stables, dining tent, and post office (Fleming 2016).

On 31 March 1887, the show sailed for England again.

Their ship sailed up the Thames River to the Gravsesends in May 1887, and then traveled by rail to Earls Court, the West End of London, where the ground had been graded smooth with seven acres fenced for the show. A canvas city went up, tepees and all, in a grove of newly planted trees (Fleming 2016).

The Prince of Wales, his wife and 3 daughters visited

on 5 May with a large party of lords, ladies, dukes, and earls. Fours days after that the show opened with thousands waiting to enter. That month the show sold a half million tickets. The Queen traveled in public, for the first time since her husband's death in 1861, to watch the show, *Queen Victoria's Golden Jubilee,* from the royal box. The show gave two performances a day, six days a week, for six months with a final performance in London on 31 October 1887. For six more months they toured England, and then sailed to New York City (Fleming 2016).

On 31 May 1888 the show opened at the camp on Staten Island, leased for one month with an audience of twenty thousand.

The next year the show headed back to Europe, this time to open at the World's Fair in Paris on 19 May, 1889. From there it was Barcelona, Spain, where they ran into the flu epidemic, then on to Naples, Italy. where they met local outbreaks of smallpox and typhoid. The show announcer and five Indians died. The show traveled to Germany, making their winter quarters in Strasbourg, Germany. By this time all the Indians had returned to The United States. New ones traveled to Germany with Cody, who had traveled to the United States to solve that problem, returning with 23 Indians. While Cody was gone Nate Salsbury, Cody's partner, had organized a new show the *Congress of Rough Riders of the World:* which included: Russian Cossacks, Argentine gauchos, and English and German cavalry. With Cody's return it was merged with the wild west show which now had 650 people (Fleming 2016).

When they returned to the United States the show

opened adjacent to the official grounds of the Chicago's 1893 World's Columbian Exposition in Chicago. It was renamed *Buffalo Bill's Wild West and Congress of Rough Riders of the World,* enhancing the shows popularity.

Cody was instrumental in settling the Big Horn Basin of Wyoming. In 1896, he and six other men founded the town of Cody first named "Shoshone" which the U.S. Postmaster rejected. Cody spent a fortune trying to make the town a success, seeing it as a way to retire from show business (Fleming 2016, Warren 2005).

The term *Rough Rider* was appropriated by Theodore Roosevelt (1898) during his Cuban campaign (McMurty 2005).

With the shows manager, Nate Salsbury sick, Cody formed a business partnership with James Bailey, who had worked for P. T. Barnum as a junior partner. Bailey used his experience with Barnum and put the show on the rail, soon traveling over 9,000 miles in 190 days stopping at 131 cities. This system was utilized for the years 1895-1899. The show required three trains to move everything, including almost 23,000 yards of canvas and 20 miles of rope. Bailey added a circus-style sideshow. The show traveled 11,100 miles in 1899. The show now employed around 500 people (Fleming 2016, Warren 2005, McMurty 2005).

Cody, in partnership with "Pawnee Bill" Lillie, decided to have a two-year Farewell Tour in 1908. He extended it for an additional year as his non-Wild West show debts kept piling up. His creditors foreclosed on the show on 21 July 1913(Fleming 2016).

Cody then tried working for the *Sells-Floto Circus,*

formed by Harry Heye Tammen and Frederick Gilmor Bonfils in 1902. They hired Cody for the 1914-1915 season. Then in 1916, the *Millers Brothers 101 Ranch Wild West* hired Cody for a World War I recruitment show, the *Pageant of Preparedness*. Cody quit soon after that.

On 3 January 1917, Cody, in ill health, took the train to Glenwood Springs, Colorado. On 10 January he died and was buried on top of Lookout Mountain, 20 miles from Denver (Fleming 2016).

If one does a search for "Wild West Shows" numerous web-pages will turn up with replications of the same listing. There are, usually, 39 different shows listed. In some cases a movie is listed. Of the 39 only 14 have any information about them.

Hardwick's Great Rocky Mountain Show (1884).

Tom W. Hardwick and William Skeigle organized their show, originally called the *Great Wild West Show*, while in Deadwood. They started their tour as early as May 1884. Hardwick had been deputy Sheriff in Deadwood where he met Calamity Jane who joined the show in late June or early July. A headliner for the show was John "Liver-Eating Johnson, who allegedly ate the livers of some Indians who had killed his family. Newspapers often called the show the *Calamity Jane-Liver Eating Johnson Combination*. Hartwick had been a buffalo, wolf, and other large game hunter, an army scout, interpreter of several Indian languages, and had in his travels met William Cody, James Butler Hickok, and W. F. "Doc" Carver as well as General George Armstrong Custer.

He had spent two years in prison in Helena for violating border agreements by chasing Indians who stole his horses into Canada and attacking their camp. His show advertised on June 3, 1884 that it was *"a vivid and thrilling illustration of wild western life with one thousand men, women, Indians, squaws and animals connected with this show as well as Curley, the only survivor of the Custer massacre."* By the time the show made it to Chicago they had run out of money and the members had to sell their horses in order to get back to Montana (Herda 2019, McLaird 2005).

The Great Pawnee Bill Shows. The Only Genuine Wild West (1888-1903)

Pawnee Bill (Gordon W. Lillie), born 14 February 1860, Bloomington, Illinois, was first exposed to the Wild West show business when he served as an interpreter for the Pawnee Indians for Buffalo Bill's first show in 1883 and given the nickname "Pawnee Bill." He launched *Pawnee Bill's Historical Wild West Exhibition and Indian Encampment* in 1888. In 1889, he established *Pawnee Bill's Historical Wild West Indian Museum and Encampment,* starring May Manning Lillie as a sharpshooter. The rough-riding talents of Lulu Parr and her skill with the gun caught the attention of Pawnee Bill, who signed her to his show in 1903. Five years later, she toured with another group in Europe but came back to work for Pawnee Bill in 1911; by then, his program had joined that of Buffalo Bill's. The Metropolitan Colored Amusement Company of Louisville Kentucky, signed with the show for an opening on 14 February 1903, in Pittsburgh, Pennsylvania.

In 1907, Jose "Mexican Joe" Barrera, the *King of Mexican Rancheros*, a bronc riding and fancy roping vaquero joined *Pawnee Bill's Historical Wild West and Great Far East Show.* Barrera's daredevil performance made him one of the show's top attractions. In 1908 Pawnee Bill joined with Cody in the *Two Bills,* or, *Buffalo Bill's Wild West and Pawnee Bill's Great Far East. The* show was an economic failure. Later he bought into the Buffalo Bill show, which closed in 1913 (McCubbin and Enss 2006, Legends of America 2020b, Nichols 2010, Sampson 2014)

Congress of Rough Riders and Ropers (1899-1910)

Zachariah P. Vandeveer's parents died and he was reared by an aunt and uncle, Zack and Mary Locke Mulhall, whose family name he adopted. "Zack Mulhall," organized a troupe of Oklahoma cowhands to do trick riding and roping, bucking, horse and bronco riding, and Roman riding. He had an 80,000 acre ranch near Guthrie, Oklahoma. The show toured across the Midwest. He named the show's band, the *Frisco Railroad Cowboy Band*, after gaining sponsorship for his show from the Frisco Railroad. Mulhall had worked as a livestock agent for the St. Louis and San Francisco railway. Will Rogers, calling himself the *Cherokee Kid*, worked for the show in 1899-1900. Lucille Mulhall became the star of the show winning many of the roping contests. On 9 October 1903 in the South McAlester Indian Territory, she won over some of the best cowboys in the southwest. The show appeared in the 1904 St. Louis World's Fair. The show was at the Horse Fair at Madison Square Garden in April, 1905. In 1910 the show was named *Zack Mulhall's Wild West*. This was their last season (Rhodes 2010, Scott 1987, Rogers 1996, Enss 2016).

Buckskin Bill's Wild West (1900-1902?)

Fletcher, Ed C., John B., and Sid (or {Syd}) Terrell organized a show around a fictional character Buckskin Bill who was somewhat similar to but younger than Buffalo Bill. Buckskin Bill was played by W.F. "Harry" Brandon (1900), Victor F. Cody (1901), and "Cherokee Bill" Cahoon (1902). It opened 5 May 1900 in Paducah and traveled to Maysville, Kentucky; Chicago; Nashville, Tennessee; and Grande Rapids, Michigan; as well as other cities. They had their home quarters in: Paducah from 1900-1902; Chicago in 1903; and Forth Worth, Texas in 1904. The show included Indians, cowboys, Mexicans, Cossacks, Arabs, cavalry dressed as U.S. Military, Germany, France, and England. In 1902 the show was sold to Chicago businessmen Henry. E. Allot, J. C. O'Brien, and Val Hoffman. They changed the name in 1903 to *Buckskin Bill's Historic Wild West*, and in 1904 to *Consolidated Congress of Wonders* (Westerntrips 2014, Parker 2015).

Luella Forepaugh-Fish Wild West Show (1903).

Luella Forepaugh became the manager of *Forepaugh's Family Theatre*, a repertory theater in Philadelphia, 1895. In 1897, she and George F. Fish wrote a new adaptation of the play, the Strange Case of Dr Jekyll and Mr Hyde. Forepaugh and Fish married in 1899. They left the theater to start the *Luella Forepaugh-Fish Wild West Show*, opening in St. Louis, Missouri on April 17, 1903.

Religious Telescope (1903) wrote:

> Judge Dunwiddle, of Janesville, Wisconsin, has appointed David W. Watt receiver for the Luelle Forebaught-Fish Wild West show, which attached the owners for $23,000. The city is full of Asiatics, cowboys, negroes, and other who have not been able to raise the necessary money to leave.

Booger Red's Wild West Show (1904-1910)

Samuel Thomas Privett was born on 29 December 1858 in Williamson County, Texas, into a family of ranchers. When he was six years old, his father moved the family to Erath County, Texas and established the SP ranch. Samuel had flaming red hair and by the time he was twelve was called *that Redheaded Kid Bronc Rider*. When he was thirteen, he and a friend decided to make their own Christmas fireworks by packing a tree stump with gunpowder and lighting it off. The blast badly burned his face. Another kid looked at his face and apparently said, *Gee, Red sure is a booger now, ain't he?* The damage to his face had him saying that he was *Booger Red, the ugliest man alive.* By the time he was fifteen, after his father died, he was riding broncos on the big ranches in Tom Green, Coke, and Runnels counties of West Texas Eventually he earned enough money to purchase his own ranch near San Angelo, Texas. He married Mollie Webb, an expert horsewoman, in Bronte in 1895 and eventually had six children. He started his own show and was the star attraction. He was considered the greatest bronc rider in the world. His show grew to over 32 wagons, 22 bucking horses, and a dozen or so cowboys and cowgirls. He discovered Bill Pickett as a child, who became a famous bulldogger. He asked Pickett's mother, a former slave, for permission to take him on the road. Picket left the show in 1905 to join the *Miller Brothers 101 Ranch Real Wild West* show. Privett's show opened and closed its season in San Angelo. By 1912, Booger Red's popularity had outgrown him so he changed from running his own show to working for other wild west shows. He sold his show to the Miller Brothers. He died in March of 1924 from Bright's Disease, a kidney disease (Olson 2014, Miracle 2015, Fowler 2008, Untiedt 2013, Carlson 2006).

Colonel Cummins' Wild West Indian Congress and Rough Riders of the World (1904-1914)

Fred T. (often called "Colonel,") Cummins' show specialized in showcasing Native Americans through his close connections to the Bureau of Indian affairs. He sometimes had up to fifty different tribes and individuals such as: Nez Perce Chief Joseph, American Horse, and Oglala Sioux Chief Red Cloud and Seven Rabbits. The show consisted of showing life on the plains as they saw it, target and trick shooting, attacking settlers, demonstrations of riding and trick riding mastery, and lassoing skills. He started at the 1904 St. Louis Fair with his first named show called the *Cummins' Wild West Indian Congress & Rough Riders of the World*. In 1905 the show in Chicago as the *Cummins' Wild West and Indian Congress, Custer's Massacre and Siege of Fort Dearborn*. They advertised 850 "Indians, Mexicans, Russians, Cowboys, Japanese, Lady Rifle, Roping and Riding Experts" and a "grand Sham Battle Each Performance." In 1904 he had two silent partners, Walter L. Main and George S. Satterly. The show traveled by rail in 1905-1906, with cars outfitted for promoters, horses, circus animals (including 1 elephant car), and four wild west and Indian cars. From 1906 to 1909 it was generally referred to as *Cummins' Wild West*. By 1910 the Colonel had joined forces with Vernon C. Seavers to have the *Young Buffalo Wild West* show, previously called the *Lone Bill Wild West* show. They stayed in business together through 1914 until creditors filed for bankruptcy in Queens County, New York (Cline 2008, Rogers 2000).

Buckskin Ben's Wild West and Dog and Pony Show (1908-1929)

Benjamin M. "Buckskin Ben" Stalker convinced his wife, Mary Belinda Elder, to become skilled with the rifle and take part in his *Human Impalement Act*, throwing knives, outlining her profile. Each show ran six to eight half-hour acts beginning with the popular *Buckskin Ben Family Band* consisting of Father Ben (trombone), Mother Mary (euphonium), Alice (tuba), Jennie (trombone), Charles Davis (Alice's husband, drums), Myrtle and Ella (alto horns), George (cornet) and Noah Waddell (Ben's trick-rider sidekick, cornet). Along with "wild west" skills of bronco riding, they had sharp-shooting, throwing knives, and amusing acts of dogs and ponies. By May 1907 the show added lassoing and a monkey act. By 1908 the act had expanded so much that the family settled in Cambridge City, Indiana. He changed the show's name from *Buckskin Ben's Wild West* to the *Buckskin Ben Family Show* in 1903 and from 1908 to 1910 to *Buckskin Ben's Wild West and Dog and Pony*

Show.

Billboard (1908) wrote that:

> The Buckskin Ben Show is making a decided hit at Luna Park, Cleveland, O. The engagement at Luna was for two weeks, but owing to turn away business they have been offered an additional four weeks.

In 1910 he purchased two railroad cars: one for the family, one for their equipment. Ben retired at the age of 86 in 1929. (Wonning 2019, Holman 2017).

Miller Bros. 101 Ranch Wild West Show (1907-1916; 1926-1931)

Colonel George Washington Miller had a ranch of 1,100,000 acres spread across four counties, leased from the Quapaw Indians in the Indian Territory of Oklahoma in 1893. In 1905, the Miller Brothers, Joe, Zachary, and George Lee, put on *Oklahoma's Gala Day* of western skills and horsemanship which they called a roundup rather than a rodeo, including Tom Mix and Buffalo Bill, and invited the National Editorial Association to come. They took their show, *Miller Bros. 101 Ranch Wild West Show*, on the road, starting at Brighton Beach, New York in 1907. They shut down during World War I and then began touring again in 1926. They traveled on thirty railroad cars. Their private car had baths, electric lights, a library and other conveniences. The Miller Brothers created the *Bison 101 Film Company* with Thomas Harper Ince, the most wealthy and powerful movie producer of the time.

Their ranch had been used for making westerns, but the weather was not conducive to year round filming so they bought a second ranch in Southern California for year round shooting opportunities, more hours of sunlight, and a wide variety of landscapes and backdrops. Ince bought the ranch in California in 1912, hired on the entire 101 cast, and built a wild west movie studio set known as "Inceville," producing around 140 films a year. This made California the geographical center of the American film industry, and ushered in the Golden Age of major motion picture studio productions. In 1931 the Miller Brothers show and Oklahoma ranch was sold at auction (n.d 4, n.d 5, Miracle 2015, Wallis 1999).

Jones Bros.' Buffalo Ranch Wild West (1910)

Martin Downs owned the *Cole Bros. World Toured Shows*. He died in 1909 and his show was auctioned in 1910. J. Augustus Jones bought a ticket wagon, calliope, bandwagons, chariots, cages, three tableaux wagons, railroad cars, and baggage stock. Jones toured with a 14-car railroad show, *Jones Bros. Buffalo Ranch Wild West Show*. He sold the show to Thomas Wiedemann who toured in 1911 as the *Kit Carson Buffalo Ranch Wild West Show*, a combination circus and wild west show. The show was sold by creditors starting in 1914.
(Bradbury 1957).

California Frank's All-Star Wild West (1910)

Frank C. Smith aka C. F. "California Frank" Hafley, featured women in his rodeo as well as a sharpshooting comedy in which Lillian Smith, *The California Girl, The California Huntress and Champion Girl Rifle Shot*, a former competitor of Annie Oakley's and Hafley's first wife, Smith, shot targets from the mouth or head of Mamie Francis, Hafley's second wife. Smith also shot out a candle flame, trimmed the ash from Hafley's cigar, broke a small ball attached to his hat, and then, a dime held in his fingers. She was an outstanding shot with the rifle, shotgun, and revolver. Hafley had a hit horse-diving act, combining beautiful women, danger, and the allure of the *Wild West*. Horse diving required such a high degree of risk for both the horses and riders, it was rarely tried in most shows. Mammie Francis dove her white Arabian horse from about 50 above the tank of water. She insisted that she was a normal western girl, thoroughly prepared for her act by having busted broncos along with the men (Shoshi 2018, Scofield 2015, NYDM 1908).

Arlington & Beckman's Oklahoma Ranch Wild West (1910-1913)

A lithograph, dated 1910, announced this show along with *Frank's All Star California Wild West*. In 1913 the tent was a three-middle-pole tent with two inch solid steel side poles, seating over 3,000, with a sideshow, minstrel band, and the "grande finale" performance of the auto-polo game. In the evening the show utilized portable acetylene lamps of up to 500 candle power supplied by the Alexander Milburn Company, from Baltimore, Maryland. On 8 November 1913, Edward Arlington announced that the firm of Arlington and Beckmann had been dissolved. (American Engineer 1913, New York Clipper 1913, Billboard 1945)

Irwin Brothers Cheyenne Frontier Days Wild West Show (1913-1917)

Charles Burton Irwin was born on 14 August 1875. The family, Joseph Marvin Irwin, Mary Margaret Irwin, and brothers Frank and Charles, lived in Chillocothe, Missouri. The father was a blacksmith. At some point in time, Charles and Frank moved to Colorado. Eventually, over a period of time, Charles bought enough land, 25,000 acres, which he named the Y-6 Ranch, near Meriden, Wyoming. In 1913 the Irwin Brothers scheduled their own show, *Irwin Bros. Cheyenne Frontier Days Wild West Show,* approximately a month and a half before the *Cheyenne Frontier Days.* The Association for the Cheyenne Frontier Days filed suit attempting to enjoin the use of the term *Cheyenne Frontier Days.* In retaliation, the Irwins attempted to trademark the term. The Judge denied the injunction and the Irwins were unable to obtain the trademark although they continued to use it on their wagons and advertising. At the Winnipeg Horse Show in June 1913, the brothers had *Cheyenne Frontier Days Wild West,* advertised as the greatest wild west show in the world. The show utilized 3 flat cars, 5 box cars, 4 stock cars, 4 coaches, 4 sleeping cars, and 1 advance car to move everything. The show featured two bands, a calliope played by Clara Irwin (Frank's wife), two trained bison, a rodeo, and "Scout" Maish, the *Champion Roper of the World.* The show arrived at Sacramento, California on 23 July 1813, in thirty double length cars, with 800 people, 200 horses, a score of Texas steers, wild mules and trained buffalos and other attractions. The 1914 tour gathered a galaxy of stars of the riding and roping world with prize winners from the

California Rodeo, the Canadian stampedes of Calgary and Winnipeg, the Pendleton round-up, and the Cheyenne Frontier Days, along with Bee-Ho-Gray, called the champion trick roper of the world. They staged an Indian attack on their stage coach, and a wagon train, cowboy and cowgirls did a mounted quadrille. They advertised wild bucking mules, and "bronchos" that have never been successfully ridden. The show traveled through Nebraska, down to Colorado, and as far north as Canada. In 1916, the show again traveled to California. In 1917 the *Wild West Show* stored all their equipment at a baseball park (Sacramento Union 1914, Beck 2011, Branigan 2012 , Olson n.d., FAHJ 1913, Traffic Bulletin 1913).

☞ The Medicine Shows ☜

In Colonial America, patent medicine vendors often had booths in the local fairs. By 1773, laws had been passed against their excesses. By 1858, 1,500 patent medicines had been recorded with alcohol, opium and cocaine as the typical ingredients. Medicine Shows, by the late 19th century, especially flourished in the Midwest and in the rural South.

The North out-produced the South in the scope of markets and sales even though the 1890 data showed that the former Confederacy accounted for 65% of the nation's output. The elixirs and tonics being promoted were rarely patented, but were often trademarked.

Vaudeville began to dominate popular entertainment in cities and towns around 1900. In the rural areas the medicine show companies started to become less exotic (in costumes and atmosphere) replacing the Indian, Oriental, and Quaker with performances interrupted by medicine lectures and sales. Chemical patents did not come into use in the United States until 1925. The term "patent medicine" came from England where these "medicines" were provided to the Royal Family under *"patents* of royal favor." Many of these "medicines" often advertised they had "snake oil" in them which led to the term for charlatans being called "snake oil salesmen." Many of these "cures?" were laced with ample doses of alcohol, morphine, opium, or cocaine. Often they had high levels of alcohol, 12-46% (Legends of America 202c, McNamara 1995, Savitt and Young 1988).

Why were these shows so popular in terms of using patent medicines?

Costa (2015) wrote:

> . . . from the 1830s to the 1880s, was one of a worsening of the disease environment and of nutritional availability with no new technologies to improve health. The worsening of the disease environment was starkest in urban areas.

Humphreys (2009) wrote:

> Four major diseases stigmatized the American South in the nineteenth and twentieth centuries: yellow fever, malaria, hookworm, and pellagra. Each disease contributed to the inhibition of economic growth in the South, and the latter three severely affected children's development and adult workers' productivity.

> [the] triad of pellagra, malaria, and hookworm was inextricably linked with the rural poverty engendered by cotton culture and the tenant labor system that evolved to replace slavery after the Civil War. The rural farm worker had little money or access to health care, ate a poor diet, and lived in a subtropical landscape that was host to parasitic worms and mosquitoes.

> . . . pellagra is a disease caused by a deficiency

of niacin (or the amino acid tryptophan, which the body converts to niacin) in the diet. Severe cases are marked by dermatitis, diarrhea, dementia, and coma leading to death. Nearly 100,000 deaths in the United States were attributed to pellagra in the first four decades of the twentieth century, making it the most severe nutritional deficiency disease in U.S. history. Most of those deaths occurred in the South, and blacks and women bore the brunt of the disease.

The hookworm is a tiny parasite that latches onto the wall of the small intestine, secretes an anticoagulant to promote bleeding, and feeds on the host's blood. About 110 worms can consume a teaspoon of blood a day. A well-fed host with adequate iron intake can usually replace the lost iron and plasma proteins of a mild infection, but a malnourished person harboring sizable numbers of parasites will become anemic and protein deficient. In children the disease stunted physical and cognitive development. It made them weak, apathetic, and perpetually tired.

Frederickson (2016) wrote:

Tuberculosis plagued the South more than any other section of the United States and hit African Americans especially hard. Widespread poverty for generations following Reconstruction exposed hundreds of thousands of poor, rural southerners to hookworm infection and pellagra.

The medicine show was a traveling circus with vaudeville-style entertainments on a small scale, and climaxed in a pitch for some sort of cure-all nostrum. The shows had 3-4, or, up to 40 personnel from about 1870 to 1930. A show was about 45% entertainment, 45% spiel (a long or fast speech or story, used as a means of persuasion) and 10% to sell a "medicine," cure, elixir, etc. The show often completed with vaudeville-style entertainment, "Muscle Man" acts, magic tricks, and with Native American and Wild West themes. These enabled the salesman to tout the physical vigor that the product supposedly offered. This was aided by shills, who would offer "unsolicited" testimonials about the benefits of the medicine for sale. Others who had a problem, such as a limp, would shuffle forward, but only after the "Professor" gave the individual a teaspoon of his "magical elixir," was he suddenly cured right in front of everyone's eyes (Doc's Midway Cookhouse 2020a, Dead Media Archive 2010, McNamara 1995).

Baker (n.d.) noted that:

> The growth of the patent medicine industry was encouraged by a number of political, social and economic factors.
>
> Among the mundane was "dyspepsia," the 19th century's most common disease. With symptoms as varied and vague as those advertised for Dr. E. Rowell's Invigorating Tonic and Family Medicine ("For impure blood, dyspepsia, indigestion, constipation, loss of appetite, biliousness, headache,

jaundice, loss of memory, piles, eruptions of the skin, general debility, rheumatism, and all diseases arising from disordered liver, bowels or kidneys"), dyspepsia was the direct result of a poor diet. European visitors to this country universally commented on the American habit of gobbling enormous amounts of starch, salt and fat.

Adams (1907) wrote that [spelling as it was writen]:

If there is no limit to the gullibility of the public on one hand, there is apparently none to the cupidity of the newspapers on the other. As the Proprietary Association of America is constantly setting forth in veiled warnings, the press takes and enormous profit from patent-medicine advertising. Mr. Hearst's papers alone reap a harvest of more than half a million dollars per annum from this source. The Chicago *Tribune*, which reaps nostrum advertising in a spirit of independence, and sometimes with scant courtesy, still receives more than $80,000 a year in medical patronage. Many of the lessor journals actually live on patent medicines. What wonder that they are considerate of these profitable customers! Pin a newspaper owner down to the issue of fraud in the matter, and he will take refuge in the plea that his advertisers and not himself are responsible for what appears in the advertizing columns. *Caveat emptor* is the implied superscription above this department.

Dr. Ashbel P. Grinnell of New York City, who

made statistical study of patent medicines, asserts as a provable fact that more alcohol is consumed in this country in patent medicines than is dispensed in a legal way by licensed liquor venders, barring the sale of ales and beer.

Young (1960) stated that:

The two most important reasons for the rise of patent medicines were the unsatisfactory state of health in the nation, and the expansion of ways by which ailing citizens could be confronted with messages of hope.

The hope of a nation's health is never satisfactory, in that disease is never vanquished and death defeated. Since people hope for the impossible, the quack always has a potential clientele. In our own scientific age, more money is made on medical quackery than any other category of crime. In the early nineteenth century, the degree of desperation was greater, or, at least, usually came earlier and more often in the life of the average man. He was panicked by smallpox and yellow fever, but killed more often by the less dramatic respiratory and dysenteric infections. After 1815 urban mortality began to rise. Tuberculosis was on the increase, as were the dread fevers, typhoid, typhus, and yellow, and in 1831 cholera began to stalk the American landscape. Both the isolation of rural life and the tensions of urban factory labor were conducive to psychosomatic disorders.

Some of the Companies.

Hamlin's Wizard Oil Company

Founded in 1851 in Chicago by John and Lysander Hamlin, it was one of the largest, most successful American medicine shows that had a remedy for: rheumatism, neuralgia, toothache, headache, diphtheria, sore throat, lame back, sprains, bruises, corns, cramps, colic, diarrhea, and all pain and inflammation, claimed to contain 50-70% alcohol, camphor, sassafras oil, clove oil, turpentine, ammonia, and chloroform. His income allowed John Hamlin to buy the Chicago Grande Opera House (McNamara 1995).

The Kickapoo Indian Medicine Company

It was founded by Charles H. "Texas Charley" Bigelow and John E. "Doc" Healey, a small-time New Haven peddler, in 1881. From 1881-84 the Kickapoo Indian Medicine Company was headquartered in Boston, then in New York for three years and in 1887 settled its 'Principal Wigwam' in New Haven before a final move to Clintonville, Connecticut, in 1901. The traveling medicine show featured fake war dances and marriages, dances, acrobatics, vaudeville acts, fire eaters, rifle shooting, ventriloquists and trained dog acts. They eventually had close to 100 troupes on the road at one time and traveled as far west as Chicago and as far south as the West Indies. They capitalized on the belief that the Indians had secret healing powers. They sold *Kickapoo Indian Sagwa: Blood, Liver, Stomach and Kidney Renovator* which was supposed to cure Dyspepsia, Sick Headache, Sour Stomach,

Loss of Appetite, Heartburn, Depression, Neuraliga (sp?), Female Disorders, Liver Complaint, Constipation, Indigestions, Rheumatism, Impure Blood, Jaundice, Bilious Attacks, Fever and Ague, and all Diseases of the Stomach, Liver, Kidneys and the Blood. The various active ingredients included: aloe (strong laxative), rhubarb, capsicum, mandrake (a hallucinogenic plant), guaicum (local stimulant), sal soda (for a strong alkaline taste), and alcohol (Weiser 2017, New England Historical Society 2019, Lefler 2019, McNamara 1995)

Oregon Indian Medicine Company

In 1866, Thomas Augustus Edward, born in Saugerties, New York, in 1832, was a member of the Secret Service, who traveled to Oregon during the Snake Indian War. It is suggested that the idea for Indian Medicines came to him during that time. He began to sell "Indian" medicines at the Centennial Exposition in 1876. In the same year he and his brother, Alfred, organized their company in Pittsburgh. To lend authenticity to their "Indian" remedies, the company exploited the image and reputation of Donald McKay, a Warm Springs Scout captain who had participated in the Oregon Modoc War (1872-73). In 1882 a factory was built in Corry, Pennsylvania, with full production by 1885. Their medicine show ran through the turn of the century. After Edward's death in 1904, the company was run by his daughter who sold the company to Jerry Frantz, about 1912 (Sideshow World n. d., Kook Science 2019, Biron 2013).

Dr. Cyrenius Wakefield

He was the Bloomington, Illinois, leader in the patent

medicine trade. In 1850, he and his brother, Zera Wakefield, opened a factory that began to produce: *Blackberry Balsam* [for dysentery] (12% alcohol, Blackberry root, White Oak Bark, Columbo Root, Rhubarb Root, Culver's Root, Prickly Ash Root, Catechu Gum, Potassium Carbonate, Cranesbill, Camphor); *Golden Ointment* (6% alcohol) [for burns, boils, chapped hands, hemorrhoids] (35 cents); *Cathartic Liver Pills* (podophyllum resin- a powerful laxative, curacao aloe) [liver, kidney problems, indigestion, "removing matter from the stomach and bowels"]; *Cherry Pectoral, Egyptian Salve, Golden Ointment* [for burns, boils, chapped hands, hemorrhoids, Summer Complaint {children teething}; *Rheumatic Resolvent, Worm Destroyer* [intestinal parasites]; *Worm Lozenges*; and *Wine Bitters*. By 1874 the business had forty people working with annual sales of $100,000. They used 25 tons of paper for advertising, using the usual testimonials from "satisfied" patients.(Beier 2009, Steinbacker 2008, Old Main Artifacts 2015)

George W. Merchant

Merchant started in 1871 in Philadelphia making *Merchant's Vegetable Worm Tablets*, then relocated his laboratory and office to Lockport, New York, in 1875. In 1883, he started Merchant's Gargling Oil Company, mainly for tired and sore drivers along the Erie Canal as well as the mules and horses . It was intended to cure almost any illness that the animals could have, specially for surface wounds and skin ailments. The oil ointment contained camphor, ammonia, chloroform, sassafras, cloves, and turpentine along with 50 to 70 percent alcohol and was made in two types: one for humans, one for animals (horses, cattle, sheep, poultry). For people it was supposed to be good for cramps or spasms of the stomach, colic, asthma, or internal pain, to be taken with sugar, or syrup. Merchant sold the business in 1855 to M. H. Tucker. The business ended in 1928 (Meyer V 2012, Farley 2008, Long 1993).

Lash's Bitters

In February John Spieker, a pharmacist, and Totti M. Lash, a filter manufacturer, formed a company, T. M. Lash & Co., in Sacramento, California. The net profits for the years 5 February to 4 October 1892 was $55, 872. The partnership was dissolved on 31 October 1889 with Spieker buying out his partner with the new company named Lash's Bitters Company. In 1893 the company moved to San Francisco and incorporated under the same name. The company opened offices in Chicago in 1901 and New York City in 1904. In 1914 Spieker died and his wife, Cornelia Ackley Spieker ran the company. The company finally closed in 1966 after the death of Martin O'Shea, the vice president of Lash's Bitters.

The company claimed that the Bitters cured: biliousness, malaria, dyspepsia, indigestion, chills and fever, sick headache, sour stomach, neuralgia, pain in back, and all affections of the kidneys and liver. The label stated that it was "especially adopted for women and children in habitual constipation and malaria." The principal ingredient was the back of the Buckthorn Tree, *Rhamnus purshiana*, also known as *Cascara sagrada*. It is still used for laxative properties in many herbal remedies. It also contained coriander seed, cardamon seed, cinnamon bark, licorice root, sugar, and 18%

alcohol (Torbenson et al 20011).

Dr. Tutt's Manufacturing Company

The company was located in New York and claimed that *Dr. Tutt's Liver Pills* were to be used for constipation. The pills contained a large amount of mercury, which is toxic and can cause memory problems, anxiety, hearing difficulties, and more (Lefler 2019).

H. H. Warner

The company was located in Rochester, New York, and manufactured *Warner's Safe Cure for Bright's Disease* which causes a chronic inflammation of the kidneys. The ingredients included alcohol, glycerin, and potassium nitrate (saltpeter). The potassium nitrate is contraindicated for those with renal failure (Lefler 2019).

Some of the Patent Medicines
(of the many many)

Cannabis Indica

In the 19th century cannabis was often one of the secret ingredients in patent medicines. There were at least 2,000 cannabis medicines prior to 1937, produced by over 280 manufacturers.

Peruna (Adams 1907)

This was produced by Dr. S. B. Hartman in Columbus, Ohio. It was half a pint of 190 proof alcohol, a pint and a half water, a little cubebs for flavor, and burned sugar for color. It cost 15-18 cents per bottle and sold for $1.00. It claimed to cure *catarrh*, a term that was pasted onto anything that a person might feel "ill" about: pneumonia-catarrh of the lungs; dyspepsia-catarrh of the stomach; enteritis-catarrh of the intestines; appendicitis-catarrh of appendix; Bright's disease-catarrh of the kidneys; heart disease-catarrh of the heart; canker sores-catarrh of the mouth; and, malaria-catarrh of the mosquito that bit you.

The term *catarrh* means an inflammation of the mucous membranes of the head and throat, with a flow of mucous. They advertised cures for illnesses defined as: Bronchial catarrh was bronchitis; suffocative catarrh was croup; urethral catarrh was gleet; vaginal catarrh was leukorrhea; epidemic catarrh was the same as influenza; catarrhal bronchitis is acute bronchitis (Thornber n.d.).

Bayer Heroin Hydrochloride (Heroin)

Bayer Pharmaceutical Products invented heroin (diacetylmorphine) selling it from 1898. It was promoted as a cough suppressant as well as a better and safer substitute for morphine and codeine. Bayer stopped manufacturing heroin in 1913. It was banned in the US in 1924.

Kimball White Pine and Tar Cough Syrup (Chloroform)

This contained four minims of chloroform, marketed as an effective tonic for cold symptoms and bronchitis. As early as 1847, chloroform was used to relieve asthma symptoms and as a general anesthetic. In 1976, the Federal

Drug Administration prohibited the use of chloroform for human consumption after the substance was found to cause cancer in lab animals.

Mrs. Winslow's Soothing Syrup (Morphine)

Mrs. Charlotte N. Winslow launched her Soothing Syrup in Maine in 1849. It combined sodium carbonate, aqua ammonia, and 65mg of morphine per fluid ounce. In 1911 the American Medical Association called it a "baby killer." It remained on the market in the UK until 1930.

Ergoapiol (Ergot and Apiol)

It was made from ergot (a fungus that grows on rye grain - capable of reducing blood circulation to the point of creating gangrene) and apiol (derived from celery leaves and parsley - small doses can induce abortions). It was sold in the early 1900s to treat menstrual irregularities. But taken in large quantities it could damage the liver and kidneys.

Hostetter's Bitters

32-44% alcohol (Adams 1907).

Lydia Pinkham

19-20% alcohol (Adams 1907).

Hood's Sarsaparilla

18% alcohol (Adams 1907).

Burdock's Bitters

25% alcohol (Adams 1907).

Ayer's Sarsaparilla

26% alcohol (Adams 1907).

Paine's Celery Compound

21% alcohol (Adams 1907).

Radam's Microbe Killer - Liquozone

A weak solution of sulphuric and sulphurous acids, with traces of hydrochloric and hydrobromic acid, but it was mostly water. It was created by Douglas Smith, a professional promoter, who claimed it would cure 13 different problems, from bowel problems to rheumatism and yellow fever, all alleged to be caused by "microbes." He bought out Powley's Liquefied Ozone, relocated to Chicago, and started the Liquid Ozone Company. He hired Claude C. Hopkins, Advertising Manager, to leave Dr. Shoop's Restorative and work for Smith (Adams 1907).

Orangeine

Does not contain anything derived from an orange but is a mixture of acetanild and other less potent drugs. Acetanilid thins the blood, depresses the heart, and undermines the entire system. It was supposed to cure nervousness and headaches (Adams 1907).

Miniature Headache Powers

It was a mixture of salicylate of soda and milk sugar (Adams 1907).

Dr. William's Pink Pills for Pale People

A mixture of green vitriol, starch, and sugar that was supposed to cure paralysis (Adams 1907).

Dr. John Hooper's Female Pills

These were supposed to cure giddiness [a reeling or whirling sensation], poor digestion, a "dejected countenance," a dislike of exercise and conversation. The ingredients were dried sulphate of iron, powdered senna (a laxative), powdered canella (tree bark), powdered jalap (dried root of Ipomoea purga), aloes, oil of pennyroyal, and "excipient" with the effective ingredients largely being strong laxatives (Lefler 2019).

Coca-Cola

Dr. John Pemberton, Atlanta pharmacist, formulated, in 1886, a drink with a small amount of cocaine as a "brain tonic and intellectual beverage" that might also relieve menstrual distress. The cocaine was replaced in 1903 by a non-narcotic extract from coca leaves, but an entire generation had grown up on the fortified beverage used as a tonic (Long 1991).

Atkinson and Barker's Royal Infants' Preservative

Babies were spoon-fed this drug. The advertisement for *Atkinson and Barker's Royal Infants' Preservative* claimed relief for teething pain, bowel problems, flatulence and convulsions. It also said that laudanum was "no stupefactive, deadly narcotic" but rather a "veritable preservative of infants." Stupefactive is a drug inducing unconsciousness or insensibility. The ad failed to mention that, besides its addictive properties, laudanum can cause constipation, itching, respiratory distress, and constriction of the pupils. Although it is still available, its use is restricted both in the US and UK. Laudanum is an alcoholic extract containing around 10 percent powdered opium. As early as 1676 it was promoted as a remedy for various conditions, and by the 1800s it was used to treat everything (Amondson 2013).

Norodin

It was the brand name for methamphetamine. The advertisement claimed that it was "useful in dispelling the shadows of mild mental depression" and that it has "relatively few side effects." However, it can result in various physiological effects, including anorexia, tooth grinding, irregular heartbeat, insomnia, abnormal blood pressure, heart attacks, and strokes. It is also extremely addictive and is one of the hardest dependencies to overcome. Surprisingly, methamphetamine is occasionally used today as a treatment for ADHD and obesity (Amondson 2013).

Snake Oil

Snake oil was extracted from the oil of Chinese water snakes and arrived in the United States with the influx of Chinese workers toiling on the Transcontinental Railroad in the 1880s. Rich in omega-3 acids, it was used to reduce inflammation and treat arthritis and bursitis, and was rubbed on the workers' joints after a long day of working on the railroad. Clark Stanley, "The Rattlesnake King" claimed to have studied with a Hopi medicine man who turned him on to the healing powers of snake oil. He labeled his patent medicine snake oil although it didn't contain any kind of snake oil, rattlesnake or otherwise.

The Pure Food and Drug Act of 1906, along with the advent of the motion pictures, put a slow end to the traveling medicine show. Cocaine was banned in the U.S. in 1920.
(Lefler 2019) noted that:

> The last traveling medicine show ended in 1951 for an elixir named Hadacol. The entrepreneur Dudley LeBlanc marketed the elixir as a panacea for epilepsy, cancer, and other ailments. The elixir's name was Hadacol because LeBlanc "had to call" it something. Hadacol contained B vitamins, alcohol, and diluted hydrochloric acid. He toured the country with celebrities and was the second biggest advertiser in the country. The Hadacol enterprise fell apart when the public found out LeBlanc was in trouble with the IRS and the company was in debt.

Patent medicine is still available today. Herbal manufacturers make many unsubstantiated claims as long as they place this FDA caveat somewhere upon the label: "This statement has not been evaluated by the Food and Drug Administration. This product is not intended to diagnose, treat, cure, or prevent any disease."

☞ The Minstrel Shows ☜

Williams 2020) stated that:

> The American minstrelsy borrows from opera,
> English farce, Shakespeare's plays, and Irish
> jigs. It also borrows from such African
> American forms as the juba, the knock Jim
> Crow (a children's game), the ring shout
> (sacred ritual), and the cakewalk. One could
> even find the striking poses of Josiah
> Wedgwood's anti-slavery medallions on the
> minstrel stage.

Grosvenor and Toll (2019) wrote that:

> . . . minstrel shows were more popular in the
> North than Dixie, especially in urban areas.
> The audiences were "large, boisterous, and
> hungry for entertainment," says Toll. "They
> hollered, hissed, cheered, and booed with the
> intensity and fervor of today's football fans."

> The minstrels had a long-lasting impact, with
> cruel stereotypes that echoed in popular
> culture for 150 years. Abolitionist Frederick
> Douglass decried blackface performers as "the
> filthy scum of white society, who have stolen
> from us a complexion denied to them by

nature, in which to make money, and pander to the corrupt taste of their white fellow citizens."

Toll (1978) wrote:

> From Aunt Jemima to Mammy in Gone With the Wind, from Uncle Remus to Uncle Ben, from Amos 'n' Andy to Good Times, the inexplicably grinning black face is a pervasive part of American culture. Only recently have black performers been able to break out of the singing, dancing, and comedy roles that have for so long perpetuated the image of blacks as a happy, musical people who would rather play than work, rather frolic than think. Such images have inevitably affected the ways white America has viewed and treated black America. Their source was the minstrel show.

The caricatures utilized in the minstrel shows tended to conform to one or more of the following stereotypes (ODB n.d.):

> *Jim Crow* – the term originated in 1830 by Thomas "Daddy" Rice, who blackened his face with burnt cork and danced a jig singing the song, "Jump Jim Crow;"
> *Zip Coon/Dandy Jim* – created by George Dixon, in 1834, to make a mockery of free blacks, was a northern, urban, sartorially splendid dandy, dressing in high style and

speaking in a series of malaprops and puns that undermined his attempts to appear dignified;

Mammy – a source of earthy wisdom who is fiercely independent and brooks no backtalk. Billy Kersands wrote in 1875, a song "Aunt Jemima" for a white minstrel artist in 1875. It was heard by Chris Rutt in 1889, who trademarked the name, and sold it to The Davis Company, who in 1893, hired Nancy Green, a former enslaved woman, to sell pancakes at the Chicago Exposition (USF n.d2);

Uncle Tom – typically good, gentle, religious and sober, another favorite of advertisers such as "Uncle Ben" still using the face to sell rice. *Uncle Tom's Cabin* was published in 1852;

Buck – a large black man who is proud, at times menacing, always interested in white women;

Wench/Jezebel – a temptress, typically a male in female garb, in movies, female mulattos, a "nigger wench," white male-as-black male-as-black female (Cockrell 1997);

Mulatto – mixed-blood male or female, often portrayed in movies as a tragic figure, passing as white, intentionally or unintentionally, until they are discovered to have black ancestry. The name "Hannah, often referred to in songs," is about a mulatto woman, usually sexually desired, symbol of master-on-slave sexuality (USF n.d2);

Pickaninny – children with bulging eyes, unkempt hair, red lips and wide mouths, often eating huge slices of watermelon.

Jim Crow and **Zip Coon** merged into *"coon."*

Watkins (1994) wrote:

> Around 1828 . . . George Washington Dixon introduced "Coal Black Rose," a comic song about a Negro woman and her rival lovers (Sambo and Cufee), to American audiences. The song ridiculed the lovers' vows of affection and ended with a burlesque confrontation in which loves turns to hate. With Dixon's performances of this and other minstrel songs at circuses and variety shows in New York, his popularity increased significantly.

> George Nichols, another circus clown, began doing blackface impersonations in the 1820s and claims to have written "Zip Coon" (now popularly known as "Turkey in the Straw"), although Dixon and another blackface performer, Bob Farrell, known as "Zip Coon," also claimed authorship of the song. Some show business historians even contend that Nichols originally introduced "Jim Crow" – a tune that, when brought to the stage by another performer, almost singlehandedly catapulted blackface acts into national prominence.

Thomas Dartmouth "Daddy" Rice, a blackface performer, claimed that he saw, ca. 1828, while visiting Louisville, Kentucky, a crippled black stablehand singing the song "Jim Crow" to himself and dancing a shuffling, hopping dance. Rice's first performance was on 22 September 1830, between performances of two serious dramas: *The Hunchback* and *Catherine of Cleves* His dance was a variation of the shuffle where the feet remain close to the ground with an upper-body movement predominating. He wrote new verses for the lyrics of "Jim Crow." His performance became an immediate hit along the Ohio River Valley. Rice and other performers, Nichols, Farrell, Ben Cotton, and J. W. Sweeny, called themselves "Ethiopian Delineaters," performing during their tours what they claimed were authentic Negro songs and dances (Watkins 1994, Koenig n.d.).

Kaufmann (1937) wrote that:

> Rice was not the first Negro impersonator, although the first to cut any kind of a swath. The dignified Gottlieb Graupner, father of the Boston symphony Orchestra, is said to have appeared in black face in 1799 and again ten years later as a dark entertainer for light moments. On the first occasion, he sang The Gay Negroe Boy in Act II of Oronooko, accompanying himself on the banjo. Another gentleman known as Pot-Pie Herbert followed his example. Black clowns were an accepted part of circuses of the early nineteenth century, while between-the-acts diversions of Negro song and dance were used to save ponderous dramas from failure.

Toll (1978) points out that:

Before the Civil War, American show business virtually excluded black people. But it never ignored black culture. In fact, the minstrel show—the first uniquely American entertainment form—was born when Northern white men blacked their faces, adopted heavy dialects, and performed what they claimed were black songs, dances, and jokes to entertain white Americans. No one took minstrel shows seriously; they were meant to be light, meaningless entertainment.

Before the Civil War between acts of plays there were performers who drew heavily on American folklore and folk song to entertain the audiences. As blacks were rarely allowed to do this, white men wearing burnt cork make-up provided the entertainment (Toll 1978).

Cockrell (1997) wrote [terminology as written]:

Early minstrelsy's music (or its noise) jangled the nerves of those who believe in music that was proper. Respectable, polished, and harmonic, with recognizable melodies. "Jim Crow" was not at all the way music was supposed to be: It was music for the croaking voice and the wild fiddle; the tune is awkward, repetitive, and even boring; the texts are disjointed, generally nonnarrative, and unrealistic. This music assaulted sensibilities, challenged the roots of respectability, and promised subversion, a world undone, and, concomitantly, a new set of codes.

Davis (2000) felt that:

The form was so natural, it seemed improvised – and, in fact. much of the evening, because of the talents of the four, was. But most of all, there was exuberance and excitement. The minstrels, in their wide-eyed, large-lipped, ragged-costumed absurdity, rolled onto the stage in a thundercloud of energy which hardly ever dissipated. They insulted each other, they baited each other, they made mincemeat of the language, they took the audience into their fun, and, in one night, they added a new form to show business in America – in fact, the world.

It was suggested (USF n.d3, n.d4) that:

Blackface allowed actors and artists to hide behind a caricature while protesting and mocking the powerful without fear of retaliation. Minstrel performers could safely question authority while claiming to be acting out authentic African American expressions.

The exaggerated features of his disguise bear all the marks of a counterculture: he is not only poor, but his extremities and facial features protrude in ungainly ways meant to confront the smooth regularity of idealized gentility.

Blackface would always be Janus-faced, allowing the artist to speak freely against the interests of the powerful, a potent symbol of Jacksonian democracy. On the other hand, blackface dangerously dehumanized blacks by introducing and reinforcing racial stereotypes.

Blackface popularized inaccurate
representations of blacks while preventing
blacks from representing themselves.

. . . after the Civil War, blackface characters
were cast as simpletons longing for easy lives
on a plantation. In many variations, an elderly
ex-slave longed to return to his master's
plantation to rest his bones before he died.
These aged characters also implicitly longed
for the supposed safety and stability provided
by the rigid racial hierarchy of yore.
Emancipation had ushered in uncertainty and
racial violence. Returning to the plantations
could turn back the clock to a mythical simpler
time, and at least according to some white
songwriters, a happier time.

Kaufmann (1937)wrote that:

Under the rough and ready, catch-as-catch-can
technique of the minstrel show, American song
assumed a special character. Wholly apart
though it was from the field of art song, and
remote as the minstrel band was from the
symphony orchestra, there was, nevertheless,
an interaction between the two. The same
audiences listened to both. The wise composer
took heed of both. And many of the true Negro
songs were poured through the funnel of the
minstrel show into that dilute, composite fluid
known as American music, bringing to it
sentiment, humor, and the beginnings of
ragtime and jazz.

By the 1840s, the show typically was divided into two parts: the urban black dandy and the southern plantation slave. They often included a Master of Ceremonies, Mr. Interlocuter, and two clowns: Tambo and Bones (Williams 2020).

In the late 1850s most of the minstrel shows followed the same structure of three-acts. The walkaround was the entire company dressed in flashy clothes and exaggerated makeup singing some popular song ending in a rousing song or a love ballad. This was followed by various performances including a stump speech which was a speech filled with puns. The last was a slapstick plantation skit with lots of music, sometimes poking fun at some popular play (Cockrell 1997). The minstrel show's message was that black people belonged only on Southern plantations and had no place at all in the North (Toll 1978).

It has been suggested that the Panic of 1837 reduced theater attendance and that the growth of the minstrel show entered as a replacement with over 5,000 traveling minstrel shows and circus shows from 1850 to 1853. Ten theaters in New York had minstrel shows in the 1850s (Carlyon 2001, Mandell 2019).

Minstrel shows became the first distinctly American theatrical form by removing 19th Century Victorian conventions. Minstrel songs ranged from racial lampoons to political satire to treacly 19th century sentimentality. (USF n.d1, Lott 2013, Koenig n.d.).

Mandell (2019) pointed out that:

> As early as the 1840s, minstrel shows made stars out of such African-American entertainers as Thomas Dilward, and William Henry Lane, nicknamed Master Juba, who toured with the otherwise all-white Ethiopian Minstrels billed as the "Greatest Dancer in the World." Lane is considered the father of tap dance.
>
> For all its perpetuation of false and debilitating stereotypes, the minstrel show made concrete contributions to American popular arts. Although the minstrel show as popular stage entertainment virtually disappeared a century ago, it remains a part of our cultural DNA.
>
> It was for minstrel shows that white composer Stephen Foster wrote some of his still-popular songs, such as "Camptown Races" and "Oh, Susanna," and black composer James Bland wrote hundreds of songs, including "Carry Me Back to Old Virginny," which for more than half a century was the state song of – yes — Virginia.

By this time there was a "standard" of what the show ought to look like and how it was to be performed.

The gold rush of 1852 sent blackface companies swarming to the coast, to give three shows a day, with seats selling at three dollars apiece (Kaufmann 1937).

Courtright (1901)wrote, in "The Complete Minstrel Guide:"

> For the first part, or semicircle, black dress suits are preferable, with uniform ties, wigs, shoes etc. The end men may wear ruffled shirt fronts and colored ties, comic wigs, anything to make them look eccentric. White glove should be worn by all the singers. If other suits are preferred, let white predominate, and through out the whole entertainment, if dressed in rags with only a part of a collar or shirt, let them be clean.

(Padgett n.d., In Stages 2016) noted that:

> African cultural traditions include many folk tales of trickster animals, including birds, such as crows and buzzards who seem foolish, but who always manage to get what they want through cleverness and luck. In the Yoruba culture of West Africa, he is a crow named "Jim." The slave trade brought these folk tales to America and "Jim Crow" was a favorite. Some slaves even adopted a Jim Crow type attitude as a way of coping with their enslavement. They would play dumb or act the fool as a clever way of avoiding work.

> Laws were passed in the 17th Century that prohibited slaves from performing their native dances because whites believed the slave way of dancing formed a cross with their feet, something they considered blasphemous. In order to evade the law, slaves developed a shuffle dance where their feet didn't cross. They called the dance the Jim Crow.

> Jump Jim Crow began as a slave folk song, then became a

"corn song;" sung by slaves at corn huskings.

The staged character of Jim Crow came to resemble "Sambo," a "plantation darky," an uneducated rural slave, content to be living on a plantation. The term was Spanish, "Zambo," for mixed African and American Indian people, apparently utilized as early as the 1700s (Sotiropoulos 2006, Ministrelsy n.d.).

Dumont (1899) wrote that [italics in original]:

A minstrel entertainment gives the young amateur rare opportunities to display talent in the vocal, comedy and dancing lines. No form of entertainment is so replete with comedy, noir gives such universal satisfaction when well represented. It affords vocalists a chance to *come out* in solo or concerted work, the young comedians or dancers excellent opportunities to *shine forth* and give full vent to their humor and wit. Minstrely is the one American form of amusement, purely our own, and it has lived and thrived even thought the plantation darkey, who first gave it a character, has departed. The dandy negro has supplanted him, but the laughable blunders are still incorporated in the negro of the present time. The ballads of Stephen C. Foster, breathing the slave life and the cotton fields, have been laid aside for the modern love song with a dramatic story or descriptive ballad, – yet the minstrels sing them and the change from ante-bellum days to the darkey of the present time, has been accomplished without perception. Minstrelsy is the most popular form of amusement and is always selected as a vehicle to present the talent of a club, college, school or association. With this in view, the present book is compiled . . .

Some of the Shows
(for which there is some data)

Dumont (1915) wrote that:

> It would be impossible to mention the names
> of all the new talent coming into minstrelsy
> between 1860 and 1870. Many of the troupes
> were short lived, and many good amateur
> companies finally drifted into it and became
> part and parcel of the regular organized
> troupes. Very often troupes changed titles and
> re-appeared under other names, with a
> different "angel," but always with the same
> membership.

The African Melodists

A group that claimed to represent the "colored"
population of "old Virginny." (Jackson 1967).

The Virginia Minstrels

Billy Whitlock, Frank Pellham, Daniel Decatur
Emmett, and Frank Brower (all "Ethiopian" delineators)
organized themselves as the Virginia Minstrels in the winter
of 1842-1843, aiming at the middle-class audience that would
have some interest in the exotic ways of southern blacks, and
being entertained at the same time. They offered an extended
exhibition of the "oddities, peculiarities, eccentricities, and
comicalities of that Sable Genus of Humanity." They
disbanded within the year (Padgett n.d., Cockrell 1997, Toll
1978, Koenig n.d.).

Carncross & Dixey's Minstrels

J. L. Carncross and Sam Sharply organized *Carncross & Dixey's Minstrels* in Philadelphia and opened at Sanford's Old Opera House on 14 April 1862. The show had Raymond Hitchcock and 100 "Honey Boys" presenting minstrelsy, vaudeville, burlesque, and musical comedy. The Honey Boys Minstrels were organized by George Evans. Evans and Ren Shields wrote the song "In the Good Old Summertime. Carncross left in1896. The show ran until 1908.

Christy's Minstrels

It was formed in 1883/1884 by Edwin Pearce Christy, a singer, actor, and stage producer, and George, his stepson, in Buffalo, New York. Their chief songwriter was Stephen Foster. After 25 August 1847 they specialized in Foster's music. The show popularized the "negro" stereotype in the plantation life portion that had the "peculiarities of the southern negro" such as: eating watermelons, stealing chickens, butchering language, and, the "negro wench character," who was foul tempered and often attacked her husband with a skillet. Edwin retired in 1855. George performed until he died in 1868 (Britannica 2019, Williams 2020).

Bryant's Minstrels

It was formed on 23 February 1857 by Dan, Jerry, and Cornelius "Neil" Bryant. The family name was O'Neills, the stage name was Bryant. Dan and Jerry had previously worked as minstrels. Dan Emmet, the composer, joined them in 1858, and wrote the song "Dixie" in 1859. He also wrote "Old Dantucker." Dixie was claimed to have become the Hymn of the South during the Civil War. It was premiered as "walk-around" music on 4 April 1859. The trouped lasted until 1882 (Trav 2020, Kaufmann 1937).

The Ethiopian Serenaders

Formed in the 1840s as high-class show, the show billing their production as a blackface "concert." They were sometimes billed as "The Boston Minstrels." Their first major performance, in 1844, was at the John Tyler White House as part of the *Especial Amusement of the President of the United States, His Family and Friends.* They added songs with a romantic nature and cut most of the bawdy material out. They did well until 1846 when they performed in England. By the time they returned Christy's Minstrels had gained most of their following.

Arlington's Minstrels

Billy Arlington {Valentine Burnell}, a comedian, stump speaker, and banjoist, formed in August 1862, *Arlington and Dinniker's Minstrels.* The name was changed to *Arlington's Minstrels* in September 1867. From 1871 to 1874, it was known as *Arlington, Cotton and Kemble's Minstrels.* Arlington shifted to *Emerson's Minstrels* and finished his career in 1898 with *Bartlett's California Minstrels.*

Barlow Bros' and Frost's Minstrels

Milton G. Barlow, blackface comedian, and actor, joined, in 1867, with James and William Arthur, a song-and-dance duo that called themselves the Barlow Brothers. In 1877 Barlow joined with George Wilson, George H. Primrose, and John T. West to form the *Barlow, Wilson, Primrose, and West Minstrels.*

Callender's Original Georgia Minstrels

Charles Callinder, a tavern owner, bought Sam Hague's *Slave Troupe of Georgia Minstrels* in 1872, renaming it *Callender's Original Georgia Minstrels.* The show was known widely through the mid-1870s (Toll 1978)

Haverly's United Mastodon Minstrels

Christopher Haverly, also known as, John H. "Jack" Haverly started his group in 1877 with 40 performers. Haverly, considered the last of the great minstrel impresarios, bought Charles Callender's *Original Georgia Minstrels,* renaming it *Haverly's Colored Minstrels* in 1878, and ran two shows independently. He had a brass band adding a drum corps in 1878. Charles Frohmnan, manager, was in charge as the show toured the United States and Europe. As a theater manager and producer Frohman produced over 700 shows. He borrowed P.T. Barnum's technique for promotion and stressed "extraordinary excellence, merit, and magnitude." The production was staged with lavish scenery and three acts. The last act was pure circus. *The Colored Minstrels* was sold to Charles and Gustave Frohman in 1882 (Toll 1978, Koenig n.d.).

West's Big Minstrel Jubilee (Primrose & West's Minstrels)

The show was produced with George Primrose, in 1877, and advertised itself the Richest and Costliest Minstrel Organization in Existence, attempting to be an even bigger extravaganza than *Haverly's United Mastodon Minstrels* which they advertised as "Our Double Company." They began to perform without blackface make-up. "We were looking for novelty," recalled George Thatcher, a star of that troupe, "and for a change tried white minstrelsy" with the cast in "Shakespearian costumes." James Bland composed over 700 songs. He joined this show with "Carry Me Back to Old Virginny" and premiered "In the Evening By the Moonlight" with both President Grover Cleveland and General Robert E. Lee in the audience. In 1882, the show did away with plantation and blackface material completely replacing it with such upper-class pursuits as fox hunting, lawn tennis, and yacht racing (Toll 1978, Koenig n.d.).

Rabbit Foot Minstrel Company

Patrick Henry "Pat" Chappelle commissioned Frank Dumont in 1900 to write a comedy-based show *A Rabbit's Foot* for a touring company. The show would include minstrel performances, dancers, circus acts, comedy and musical ensemble pieces and be owned and operated totally by an all black cast. The company had a brass band and had by 1904 had expanded to fill 3 railroad cars. The show dominated the southwest and southeast areas of the U.S. and was advertised as "The Leading Negro Show in America." It ran through the 1940s, perhaps until 1959 (Showmen's Museum 2014).

Silas Green Minstrels

"Eph" Williams, the first black circus owner, set up his show in 1885, and ended in 1902. He toured as *Prof. Eph Williams Famous Troubadours.* Around 1922 he sold a half interest to Charles Collier who ran the tour until the late 1950s. A poster advertised "Here Today. Silas Green Minstrels" (Showmen's Museum 2014).

White Gloves

Caswell (2017) wrote:

> This rubber hose and circle aesthetic that dominated early animation posed a problem for animators in the age of fuzzy black and white film. Yes, simplifying the features of characters made the process easier and faster. However, it made it more difficult for the audience to see characters' black hands against their black bodies. Enter those crisp white gloves. Walt Disney very well might have been the first person to put white gloves on a character when he made The Opry House, starring Mickey Mouse, in 1929.
>
> As Walt Disney himself explained: "We didn't want him to have mouse hands, because he was supposed to be more human. So we gave him gloves. Five Fingers looked like too much on such a little figure, so we took one away. That was just one less finger to animate."

However one can find justification to support any kind of opinion.

Yungman (2016) argued that:

> What do Mario, Bugs Bunny, Sonic the Hedgehog, and Mickey Mouse have in common, aside from wasting countless hours of our Saturday mornings? The answer: They all wear white gloves, as do most cartoon characters you can name. But ... why? It doesn't make sense for Italian plumbers and coked-up hedgehogs to share the same fashion sense. As it turns out, it's all a big shout-out to incredibly racist minstrel shows.

☞ The Rodeo ☜

The rodeo in the United States developed out of a cowboy and cowgirl culture of the open plains, the development of cattle ranching, and the great trails traveled to deliver cattle to market. It had much to do with the western folk image that grew from those activities.

However this was not unique to the United States.

Mexico

In 1521 cattle entered Mexico with the first herd of 550 crossing the Rio Grande in what would become Texas as "meat on the hoof" for the conquistasors. In 1769 the San Gabriel mission was founded and had several hundred head of cattle that been brought earlier from Inberian Spain. The cattle were semi-wild with long horns and an irascible temper. The range cattle concept was brought into existence. By the 1530's the increase in the cattle population was almost countless. By the time period 1586-1579 some of the largest operations had 130,000-150,000 head of cattle (Felius et al 2014, Brand 1961).

The growth of ranching allowed Indians and Mestizo to become skilled horsemen and ranch hands. Due to their cultural isolation they began to develop a sense of themselves as a self-sufficient people. Over time they created their own customs, dress, and style of horsemanship called *jinetea*, a style of riding brought into Mexico from the Berber, introduced into Spain by the Moslems. This riding style was described in the Mexican literature of 1580 (LeCompte 1985).

The fiesta came into Mexico from feudal Spain and became an integral part of Mexican culture, characterized by music and dancing, fireworks, gambling, sports, and drinking, as well as prayers, masses, and the pealing church bells (LeCompte 1985).

With the expansion and development of missions in California the largest herds belonged to the missions.

By the 18th century the ranching equipment and techniques of Mexico and the Southwestern States were almost identical. In the 1830's long cattle drives were fairly common including drives from central California into northern Oregon (Brand 1961).

Brand (1961) points out that there was no Mexican literature written about the cowboy life and existence and that in Mexico the "western novel" and cowboy stories did not exist.

In California the ranch lands were fully occupied during the years 1770-1880. The breeding stock were under the care of the missions. The missions claimed most of the lands in the coastal region and had around 400,000 head of cattle and 300,00 head of sheep. Many of the solders of the time became ranchers.

In 1770, Fray Jaun Crespi of San Francisco wrote (Burcham 1961:

> The country is delightful, for it is covered with
> beautiful green grass which affords excellent
> pasture for the Animals . . .

The California prairie and oak woodland produce a plant cover with a large volume of palatable and nutritious feed. 52.7 million acres, excluding the desert lands, about 53 % of the total land area of California, was grazing land (Burcham 1961).

After 1833 the Mexican ranchos began displacing the mission ranching operations. By 1846 500 ranches operated with all but 30 having had their origin in the Mexican land grants with most of the ranch lands being former mission holdings (Burcham 1961).

Annually the herds were rounded up for branding or selecting stock for slaughter. This was call a *rodeo* (Burcham 1961).

The Spanish had large cattle-raising estates by 1528 and employed indigenous people to work as herdsmen. The vaqueros were the horsemen and cattle herders who first came to California in 1687, a horse-mounted livestock herder of a tradition that originated on the Iberian Peninsula, the hacienda system of medieval Spain, and developed in Mexico. Ranch workers, vaqueros, held informal competitions between haciendas started, prior to the Mexican Revolution, to show off the typical ranch skills such as riding and roping. The smaller landowners, rancheros or ranchers, are credited with the creation of the charreada from the charrería that had evolved from 16Th century Salamanca, Spain.

(Clayton et al 2001).

After 1821, when Mexico won their independence from Spain, the style and dress of the vaqueros became a Mexican national costume. The charreada affirmed the values of rural life. Charrería was seen as way of life outside the arena as family and social traditions, and culture. Before World War I athletes from Canada, Mexico, and the United States competed in all three countries, with little difference between the charreada and rodeo (Devlin 2020, LeCompte 1985).

Devlin (2020) suggested that the image of the charros idealized the Mexican ranch life much as Clint Eastwood and the Marlboro Man had represented the American West as a combination of valiant and skillful knight errant and cowboy galloping across move screens and in the literature as a hero of songs and at times in modern advertising.

Devlin (2020) described the costume, or *traje*, the charro wears as he performs:

> This can be a Windsor or butterfly necktie, close-fitting black trousers, gaiters, dark leather vest, and a short jacket in the same dark color, with a set of buttons and embroidered filigree. His hat is the Adalusian style, a wide-brimmed felt sombrero with thick ribbon adornments and braid in gold, silver or vivid colors. In a less formal charreada the charro might wear a simple felt or palm hat, a chamois skin jacket or shirt and chamois skin trousers with three cuff links on each side, brown or reddish brown shoes, necktie and a revolver case.

Today the charreada is divided into nine scored events called suertes. They are:

cala: individual reining competition
piales en el lienzo: roping wild mares
coleaderos: tailing wild bulls
terna en el ruedo : team bull roping
jinete de novillos: bull riding
jinete de yeguas: wild mare riding
manganas a pie: roping wild mares from on foot
manganas a caballo: roping wild mares from horseback
paso de la muerte: leaping to and riding a wild mare

Devlin (2020) pointed out that:

There are currently nearly nine hundred charrería associations in Mexico and more than one hundred and eighty in the United States. In the Southwest where Mexican Americans make up a significant proportion of the population, the charrería is relatively unknown despite the fact that charreadas are staged most Sundays from Dallas to Los Angeles.

The charrería tradition gave both Mexicans and those of Mexican descent, a source of pride. This centuries-old tradition brought together working skills, training and discipline, horsemanship, community cooperation, aesthetic expression, social protocols, gender relationships, music and dance, and the symbolic reenactment of Mexican values and activities.

Hawaii

Kamehameha I was the founder and the first ruler of the Kingdom of Hawaii. He unified the legal system and used the local products collected as taxes to promote trade with the United State and Europe. He died in May, 1819.

Kamehameha III changed the political system from an absolute monarchy to a constitutional monarchy. He balanced the process of modernization, the Western Way, while keeping his nation intact. He issued a declaration of human rights in 1839. He formalized the court system and land titles.

Captain George Vancouver, English navigator, visited the Hawaii island in 1793 and gave Kamehameha III five cattle, two ewes, and a ram. Vancouver bought the cattle from the Spanish mission in Monterey, California, before he crossed the Pacific, intending to use them as food and gifts. Before this the island had no large land mammals.

Kamehameha III imposed a *kapu*, a royal edict, forbidding anyone from hurting or killing any of these long-horn cattle. This allowed the cattle to grow in numbers until they became a major problem for the local people of Hawaii.

The cattle began digging up gardens and destroying great patches of sugarcane with their horns, beginning to threaten this part of the local economy. It was estimated that there were 20,000 cattle running loose (Wolman and Smith 2019).

In 1820 the first attempt at controlling the cattle

population was allowing men who called themselves bullock hunters to hunt them. It was essentially a waste of time and hunters.

The king then sent a royal decree to mission contacts in California requesting that vaqueros come and teach Hawaiians basic roping and the herding of cattle. The few that came brought their own well-trained mustangs and tools of the trade.

The vaqueros taught the Hawaiians how to braid four strips of rawhide into a *reata,* later called a lariat, into something that was around eighty feet long. They taught their students how to work with the horses that had been brought to the island in 1803, how to lasso and tie steers, how to break wild horses to the saddle, and how to make jerky and cure hides. The Hawaiians adopted the vaquero style of dressing but modified it to suit their own ideas of costume including redesigning the saddle and the spurs. They were called *paniolo,* a twist on the word español. The paniolo delivered horses to the ranches and cattle to the corrals at Kawaihae and other ports (Clayton et al 2001).

One of Hawaii's most famous paniolo was Eben Parker Low, born in Honolulu in 1864, spent his early years on Parker Ranch, handling cows and calves by the time he was six years old. By the time he was 26 he was the manager of Pu'uhue Ranch in Kohala, beginning a career that made him one of the most famous and colorful paniolo in Hawaii.

Bird (1875) wrote:

> . . . about 200 saddled horses were standing, each with the Mexican saddle, with its lassoing

horn, high peak behind, immense wooden stirrups, with great leathern guards, silver or brass bosses, and colored saddle cloths.

There were hundreds of native horsemen and horsewomen, many of them doubtless on their dejected quadrupeds I saw on a the wharf, but a judicious application of long rowelled Mexican spurs, and a degree of emulation, caused these animals to tear along at a fair gallop.

There were neither birds nor insects, and the only travellers we encountered in the solitude compelled us to give them wide berth, for there were a drove of half wild random cattle, led by a lean bull of hideous aspect, with crumpled horns. Two picturesque native vaccheroes on mules accompanied them, and my flagging spirits were raised by their news that the volcano was quite active. The owner of these cattle knows that he has 10,000 head, and may have a great many more. They are shot for their hides by men who make shooting and skinning them a profession, and near settlements, the owners are thankful to get two cents a pound for sirloin and rump-steaks. There are great herds which are actually wild and ownerless upon the mountains, are a degenerate breed, with some of the worst peculiarities of the Texas cattle, and are the descendants of those which Vancouver placed on the islands and which were under *Tabu* for ten years. They destroy old trees by gnawing the bark, and render the growth of young ones impossible.

On 12 August 1898 Hawaii was annexed as a territory of the United States.

In 1907 Eben traveled in the United States to visit the Cheyenne Frontier Days which attracted 20,000 people. He invited Angus MacPhee, a Frontier Days title winner, to come to Hawaii and told the newspaper he would pay the expenses of any cowboy who came as well. The Hawaiian Wild West Show started on 13 December 1907.

Cheyenne Frontier Days Secretary E. W. Stone wrote to Eben and said that they would pay travel expenses and provide room and board for a few of Hawaii's best riders and ropers to compete in the 1908 event. They should bring their own ropes and saddles, the horses would be provided. Stone said in his proposition that "We will do our best to give the boys a good time and assure them fair treatment in all contests." Ikua Purdy, Archie Ka'au'a, and Jack Low were selected to go (Wolman and Smith 2019).

Cheyenne expected about 30,000 spectators to the 1908 Frontier Days. About two days before the rodeo started the men from Hawaii received their horses.

All three were in the same activity: steer roping.

The end result of their participation in this event was a surprise to everyone other than themselves.

Ikua Purdy became the Steer Roping Champion and received a new saddle and $240. Archie Ka'au'a came in third, and Jack Low in 6th place.

It was one of the shocks to the rodeo as it was practiced and viewed in the United States at that time.

This is typified by a newspaper article from upstate

New York which stated (Wolman and Smith 2019:

For the first time in the history of the Frontier Days sports in Cheyenne, the championship for steer roping has been taken away from the United States.

It is rather galling, therefore, to have this honor taken away from us.

The other shock was Dick Stanley from Oregon who became the Broncho Busting Champion.

The Cheyenne Daily Leader wrote the headline:

WYOMING LOSES BOTH CHAMPIONSHIP TITLES.

The United States

Various comments about the early beginnings of what eventually came to called rodeo have been claimed for Santa Fe, New Mexico for 1847, Deer Trail, Colorado for 1869, and Pecos, Texas for 1883.

The claim for the Santa Fe early date(1847) is based on an account written by Captain Mayne Reid in one of his books to Samuel Arnold which stated:

Santa Fe, 10th June 1847

The town from which I write is quaint and of the Spanish style of building and reposes in a great land kissed by the southern sun. You have cows in old Ireland, but you never saw cows. Yes, millions of them here, I am sure, browsing on the sweet long grass of ranges that roll from horizon to horizon. At this time of year the cowmen have what is called the round-up, when calves are branded and the fat beasts selected to be driven to a fair hundreds of miles away.

The round-up is a great time for the cowhands, a Donneybook fair it is indeed. They contest with each other for the best roping and throwing, and there are horse races and whiskey and wines. A night in the clear moonlight there is much dancing in the streets.

Butler (2006) wrote about the author:

. . . Captain Mayne Reid was one of the most widely read authors of adventure novels in both Europe and North America. To state that his name was a household word on both sides of the Atlantic is no exaggeration. The business records of one of his principal American publishers, Ticknor & Fields, reveals that during the nineteen years from1840 to 1859 the colorful romance writer was the Boston-Based company's fifth most popular author, outsold only by Henry W. Longfellow, Josiah F. Bumstead, Sir Walter Scott, and Nathaniel Hawthorn.

Le Compte (1982) wrote about Captain Mayne Reid that:

Reid described scouting and guerilla activities around Santa Fe both in his articles for *Spirit of the Times,* and in his Mexican War novel, *The Rifle Rangers.* These descriptions are very reminiscent of his letter to Arnold, for example: " . . . the pursuit brought us to a large meadow where 500 cattle were grazing," or:

"What a glorious sunset! What a lovely land! . . . on my left waves the flag of our own land, kissed by the declining beams of the Mexican sun."

More dramatic are these lines from Chapter Ten, "Going on the scout from Vera Crus" in Reid's novel, *The Rifle Rangers:*

". . . I ascended the butte to obtain a view of the surrounding country . . . A broad belt of forest . . . swept up to the foot of the hill. Beyond this lay an open tract or meadow of prairie upon which were browsing thousands of cattle."

And further in the same book:

"At some distance from this enclosure, thousands of cattle were now browsing upon the grassy level, their spotted flanks and long upright horns showing their descent . . . Spanish bulls."

In this same chapter, Reid also mentions seeing vaqueros lassoing wild cattle and wrestling bulls to the ground by twisting their tails.

Similarities between these passages by Mayne Reid from *Spirit of the Times* and *The Rifle*

> *Rangers* and Reid's letter to Samuel Arnold
> describing the quaint town, kissed by the
> Southern sun, where there were millions of
> cattle grazing on the long sweet grass, strongly
> suggest that all three described the same town
> of Santa Fe, the one located in the state of Vera
> Cruz, in Old Mexico.

Not Santa Fe, New Mexico.

Unfortunately the misuse of a partial quote from the letter from Mayne to Butler has become a frequently repeated mythological view that seems to have taken on a life of its own. The Wikipedia *History of Rodeo* states: "Following the American Civil War, organized rodeo emerged with the first held in Cheyenne, Wyoming in 1872" citing Dirk Johnson's 1994 book *Biting the Dust* where he repeated the Captain Mayne Reid letter with no citation as to where, or from where, he heard it.

Two authors wrote about the early history of New Mexico.

Simmons (2016) wrote:

> By the 1700s the majority of New Mexicans
> lived, not on grand estancias, but on small
> subsistence farms. Their fields were unfenced
> and it was fairly simple to keep sheep away
> from the crops, since shepherds were with
> them all the time.

Raish and McSweeney (2001) wrote:

> During the Spanish Colonial (1598 to 1821) and

Mexican (1821 to 1848) periods, landownership and land use in the West were conferred by land grants from the Spanish Crown or Mexican government.

Sheep and goats were most frequently used for food. Cattle were used for plowing, threshing, transporting produce, and manuring fields.

Johnson (1994) described the life of the cowboy after the Civil War this way:

The typical cowboy worked eighteen hours a day, seven days a week. On any given day, he might be thrown from a horse or be charged by a steer. He endured the baking sun of noon, the frigid gales of darkness and the eternally whining winds that literally drove some mad. He traveled 1,000 miles with nothing more comfortable for sleeping than a bedroll. Wages for a four-month drive averaged about $100, maybe enough for a new hat and a pair of fancy boots.

In 1869 two groups of cowboys from neighboring ranches met in Deer Trail, Colorado, and decided to hold a contest to settle an argument over who was the best at performing everyday cowboy tasks, including breaking wild horses to ride. Other contestants for this event came from Hashknife, Mill Iron, and Campstool Cattle (Ordway 2002a, 2002b).

Buffalo Bill Cody on the 4th of July 1882, held the *Old Glory Blow Out*, in North Platte, Nebraska. It was a spectacle that featured fearless horseback riders, daring stagecoach drivers, and staged fights between soldiers, settlers, and American Indians. He had hoped to attract at least one hundred people to enter the contest. He got almost 1,000. Some have suggested that this event had been some type of rodeo (McMurty 2005, Fleming 2016).

The Capital State Fair, Austin Texas, started in 1875. They added the Cowboy's and Ranchman's Tournament in 1882 (LeCompte 1985).

In 1882 the now named Texas State Fair, Austin, Texas, gave a $300 dollar saddle to the cowboy who threw and tied a steer in the fastest time (Fredricksson 1985).

A bunch of cowboys, in Pecos, Texas, at Red Newell's saloon in 1883, decided to have a steer roping and bronc busting event on July 4. Local ranchers pitched in $40 in prize money (Applebome 1989).

The town of Meeker, Colorado, established in 1883, incorporated in 1885, was named for Nathan Meeker, the United States Indian Agent who was killed along with eight {some accounts state 10, or, 11} male employees by White River Ute Indians in the 1879 Meeker Massacre at White River Indian Agency. Meeker than been trying to get the Ute to convert from what he saw as their state of primitive savagery into subsistence farmers. The original structure of the White River Museum was built in 1880 as quarters for two U.S. Army officers after the Meeker Massacre and the Milk Creek Battle. The army pulled out of Meeker in 1883 and sold to the town the officers' quarters for $100 and the adobe enlisted men's barracks for $50. On the July 4th 1885 Meeker, Colorado, held its first cowboy contests during their 4th of

July celebration (Ordway 2004b). The name *Range Call* began to used in 1938.

In 1883, Trav Windham and Morg Livingston of the NA ranch both had reputations as a ropers. They decided that they would meet for a contest on July 4. As the word spread cowboys from Hashkknife Ranch, W Ranch, Lazy Y Ranch, the NA came to compete. The spot for the competition was chosen on flat land west of the river. Spectators came from all directions. Trav Windham roped and tied his steer—22 seconds—to win the roping event. Livingston beat Windham in matched roping.

Around this same time there were about fifty Wild West shows traveling from place to place.

"Arizona Charlie" Meadows and John Collins Chilson organized in August, 1884, at Mid-Town Pasture, now the site of Sawmill Crossing, Payson, Arizona, a gathering of ranchers and cowboys to engage in horse racing, bronc riding, roping events, and silver dollar pitching.

John Baumann, a British writer and travelor, came to Texas and became a "cowboy," to write about the life of the cowboy as a first-hand account. His essay (Baumann 1887) was published in the most important journal in England.

He remarked about the cowboy "myth" and his companions :

> The cowboy has at the present day become a personage; nay, more, he is rapidly becoming a mythical one. Distance is doing for him what lapse of time did for the heroes of antiquity. His admirers are investing him with all manner of romantic qualities; the descant upon

his manifold virtues and his pardonable weaknesses as if he were a demi-god, and I have no doubt that before long there will be ample material for any philosophic inquirer who may wish to enlighten the world as to the cause and meaning of the cowboy myth. Meanwhile the true character of the cowboy had become obscured, his genuine qualities are lost in fantastic tales of impossible daring and skill, of dare-devil equitation and unexampled endurance. Every member of his class is pictured as a king of Buffalo Bill, as a long-haired ruffian, who decked out in gaudy colors and tawdry ornaments, booted like a cavalier, and chivalrous as a Paladin, his belt stuck full of knives and pistols, makes the world resound with bluster and braggadocio. From this character the cowboy of fact is entirely distinct.

... my companions form a fantastic group. The well-filled cartridge-belt and heavy six-shooter, with grip menacingly protruding from its scabbard, are worn even in camp; the big Mexican spurs tinkles as their wearers move about in the long grass; the wide-brimmed sombreros cast deep shadows over sun-burned and often handsome faces, which even the stubby beard of some week's growth cannot quite disguise. Loose-throated blue flannel shirts, already in tatters, show off to advantage the well-knit frames of upright fellows in the full vigor of early manhood.

On January 30, 1886 the Dallas State Fair & Exposition was chartered as a private corporation by a group of Dallas businessmen. Another group secured a charter for a separate event, the Texas State Fair & Exposition, to open one day before the other fair. They merged in 1887 naming it the Texas State Fair & Dallas Exposition.

The Calgary District in 1886, a Canadian Pacific Railroad station, a North West Mounted Police post, and about 1000 people, held an Exhibition organized by the Agricultural Society. It was to share knowledge about practicing agriculture in the West, have fun, and showcase the best of the West. In 1908, the federal government awarded Calgary the Dominion Exhibition, a traveling fair intended to highlight the country's various regions, replacing the earlier Exhibition. Some of the entertain included the Miller Brothers 101 Wild West Show. In the spring of 1912 four men: Patrick Burns, a meat-packing tycoon and prominent rancher; A.E. Cross, the owner of the A7 Ranch and the Calgary Brewing & Malting Co, the first brewery in Western Canada; George Lane, the owner of the Bar U Ranch and an industry leader in breeding Percheron horses; and, A.J. McLean, the Manager of the CY Ranch and Member of the Legislative Assembly of Alberta, gave Guy Weadick money and tasked him with putting on the "greatest thing of its kind in the world." Weadick thought that Calgary was still firmly rooted in its *Old West* origins and that it would be the perfect place to stage a Frontier Days and Cowboy Championship Contest (Calgary Stampede 2020).

Prescott, Arizona is one of the many claiming to be the first rodeo. For the 4th of July in 1888, a group of merchants and businessmen organized a "cowboy tournament" with cash prizes. It was held on a tract of land called Forbing Park, unimproved and roped off to keep the broncs from running away if they unseated their riders. Total purses of less than $1,000 were common.

The fancy rodeo arenas that we know today were simply nonexistent in the late 1800s and early 1900s. Cowboy contests and charro fiestas were mainly folk festivals during the nineteenth century (LeCompte 1985).

Cheyenne, Wyoming, was plotted at the spot where the Union Pacific Railroad crossed Crow Creek on 5 July 1867. It rapidly grew to a population of around 4,000 people.

Colonel Slack, owner of the newspapers, the *Cheyenne News* and the *Cheyenne Leader,* met with F. W. Angier, the Traveling Passenger Agent of the Union Pacific Railroad, and, owner of a business, the Chemical Company, talked about the fact that other town had attractions that were bringing favorable attention to them as well as visitors. Agier stated that "My object is to promote passengers for the railroad by any means allowable. . . Now, I think something could be put together for Cheyenne." They felt that a day of celebration would show the life of the cowboy and cowgirl of the Wyoming plains, along with incidents of the Pony Express, stagecoach holdups, ox trains, the pioneers in covered wagons. They felt that Cheyenne could have a day that would attract people, that it would have attractions which cowboys alone could furnish, that something that few people in Denver had ever seen, with exhibitions of rough riding, bronco busting, throwing rope, and driving feats that were common to the cowboys (Kassel 2020, Flynn 1996).

The first Cheyenne Frontier Day celebration at the fair grounds went off on 23 September 1897, which was described as "wildest, crudest, most exciting and best thoroughly frontier style celebration ever seen anywhere" and that "It was only by a special dispensation of providence that a score or more of men, women, and children were not injured or killed by the action of the wild animals running through the crowds of spectators who overran the grounds" (Kassel 2020).

In 1899 Zack Mulhall, who had an 80,000 acre ranch near Guthrie, Oklahoma, organized a troupe of the Oklahoma cowhands to do trick riding and roping, bucking, horse and bronco riding, and Roman riding. His show toured across the Midwest.

Samuel Thomas Privett, who called himself, *Booger Red, the ugliest man alive,* started his own show in 1904 and was the star attraction. He was considered the greatest bronc rider in the world. His show grew to over 32 wagons, 22 bucking horses, and a dozen or so cowboys and cowgirls. He discovered Bill Pickett as a child, who became a famous bulldogger. He asked Pickett's mother, a former slave, for permission to take him on the road.

Colonel George Washington Miller had a ranch of 1,100,000 acres spread across four counties, leased from the Quapaw Indians in the Indian Territory of Oklahoma in 1893. In 1905, the Miller Brothers, Joe, Zachary, and George Lee, put on *Oklahoma's Gala Day* of western skills and horsemanship which they called a *roundup,* including Tom Mix and Buffalo Bill, and invited the National Editorial Association to come. The Miller roundup evolved into a full-fledged Wild West show. The show went on the road in 1908 moving on 16 rail cars.

Many of the touring Wild West Shows often had some

aspects of cowboy skills incorporated into the show's entertainment. The Wild West cowboys were never depicted as the manual laborers that they were, who worked the cattle on the ranches. Instead what was represented to the public were supermen with amazing skill in roping, riding, and shooting, who could perform acrobatic feats on horseback, and rescue women and children in distress (LeCompte 1985).

It has been suggested that applying the term *rodeo* to cowboy events was first used by Milt Hinkle to set his event apart from others in the Fall of 1913. (Ordway 2002).

However, Coppedge (2018) wrote that:

> Many of Hinkle's stories were true. Others might have stretched the resilience of actual fact a little bit, but were true to the spirit of the tale. And some, including the ones that have come down to us through the years, are unadulterated malarkey.

Various gatherings of cowboys had contests that were often bronc riding, bull riding, and roping contests. These gathering were mainly located at fair grounds, race tracks, and festivals of various types as well as being activities within the various Wild West shows. However, as audiences grew, promoters began to organize annual contests in specific locations as did the traveling Wild West shows.

(Pyle and Peace 2004) wrote:

> As these shows were aimed primarily at audiences in the big cities, not familiar with the West, the cowboy – or the "carnival boy" or

"bronc stomper," as he was sometimes called – stood out as a very unusual individual, coming from a background in which freedom and hardship walked hand in hand. By the late 1890s rodeo, too, had been established as public entertainment, although primarily in the western states.

The people of Pendleton, Oregon, wanted a playground, a city park. The was coupled with a desire for a real live sport, something that would put Pendleton on the map. In 1910 the creation of the Pendleton Round-Up happened as a frontier exhibition of horsemanship and cowboy skills that dazzled 10,000 spectators at its first event. Its success was the start toward having the park (Anon 1913).

When Bull Riding was introduced and irritable Brahma bulls were being used, the clowns were given the job of distracting the bull. The rodeo clown now often interposed himself between the bull and the rider, sometimes running off at an angle, throwing a hat, or shouting, so that the injured or trapped rider could exit the ring.

The cowboy contests prior to 1916 were mostly held as part of some other event, such as a fair, Wild West Show, circus, or on local ranches. It is now accepted that the western festivals and the Wild West shows were the forerunners of what became to be called *rodeo* (LeCompte 1985).

In 1919, Cody, Wyoming, had it first cowboy contest on the 4th of July. Six of Cody's leading citizens: Ernest J. Goppert, Sr., a young attorney; Irving H. "Larry" Larom, the Princeton-educated owner of a prominent dude ranch; Sid Eldred, Editor of the Park County Enterprise (a newspaper founded by William F. "Buffalo Bill" Cody); Clarence Williams and William Loewer who ran the town's small Fourth of July celebrations; and, Caroline Lockhart: a nationally best selling novelist with a flair for publicity. They had gathered to organize a new celebration, something bigger than the town had ever known, to entertain visitors driving the newly opened road to Yellowstone National Park. They felt that it should be more than a Fourth of July party, more than a cowboy contest, and more than a street dance, that is should be an event to bring back the "Old West." They called their event "the Cody Stampede" and joked that using the term "rodeo" in the title of their event "sounded like a dude word and besides we did not know how to pronounce it." They elected Lockhart the organization's president and set out to raise funds. Mary Robinson, Director of the McCracken Research Library said: "The pattern was set by Buffalo Bill's Wild West, because Buffalo Bill's Wild West brought bucking horses and made them a spectacle. He also brought women." Since then The Cody Stampeded has become a major series of events (Kudelska 2019, Clayton 2014).

LeCompte (1990) wrote:

> During the 1920s and 1930s women's competition in bronc riding, trick riding, or relay racing was included at approximately one third of all rodeos. Cowgirl events were especially popular at the most prestigious contests in the Far West, and at rodeos in major eastern cities.

More than 250 women competed in professional rodeo between 1929 and 1947, with the average career lasting over eight years.

It is also true that women's place in professional rodeo was never as secure as men's, simply because cowboys, but not cowgirls, were essential to the image of the mythical West which was the basis for the popularity of the sport.

. . . by 1943 cowgirl contests had virtually disappeared from Major rodeos.

In 1931, the Texas Cowboy Reunion in Stamford, Texas, sometime called the Stamford Cowboy Reunion, held the first sponsor contest for cowgirls. The sponsors would be the chambers of commerce throughout the region to provide girls to participate in the sponsor event at the Stamford rodeo. Each town was responsible for holding a competition to select a hometown representative with the winner competing in an event specifically designed for them. The contestants were to be judged on the appearance of their horse, their costume, and horsemanship. The original intention of the sponsor contest was to "add a little softness to the all male rodeo." In many areas the young woman who sold the most tickets, or, raised money, would become queen of the rodeo. However, the horsemanship part of the competition became increasingly popular. It had started as a subjective evaluation of the young women's ability to ride around three randomly placed barrels but turned into a timed event with a standardized cloverleaf pattern. Barrel racing became a popular and highly competitive (Laegreid 2011). Today female barrel racers are often the top money winners in professional rodeo (LeCompte 1990).

Cheyenne Frontier Days in Wyoming changed it into a selection of a young woman from within the community, and who did not compete in rodeo events, but instead used her "royal" position to promote the rodeo to a broad audience, an innovation that worked well and was widely copied (Laegreid 2011).

LeCompte (1990) noted that:

> Sponsor contexts were a major setback to women, representing all the things that female athletes have struggled to overcome, especially the emphasis on beauty and attire rather than athletic skill, and the concept that female athletes are really mere props or decorations, Rather than legitimate contestants.

> The new westerns {movies} attracted huge crowds, and had a dramtic impact on the pubic perception of the American West.

> No longer the competent, roping, riding, heroines of yore, women in singing cowboy moves were mere decorations, to be rescued by the heroic cowboys, and then won over by their songs.

> . . . women in cowboy B epics were usually not too bright, and always helpless.

In 1920, Tex Austin's World's Championship Rodeo

was held in Chicago on the lakefront, just north of where Soldier Field was to be built in 1924, in an arena which was the biggest ever built at that time. In 1922 he opened the World's Championship Cowboy Context in Madison Square Garden, New York city. It was more a sports context that a show (LeCompte 1985).

Rodeo type organizations remained fragmented until the late 1920s, when the Rodeo Association of America, comprised of rodeo committees and promoters from across the U.S., named its first champions.

The eastern indoor contests began to rival the western fiesta contests after 1922. As this continued to develop much of the early history was forgotten or ignored (LeCompte 1985).

The print media began to promote the rodeo: *Popular Mechanics* with a an article in 1926; *News Week* in 1933; *Time Magazine* in 1934. Two magazines appeared: *Hoofs and Horns* in 1931; and *Western Horseman* in 1936. This spurred an interest in rodeo which began to appear in the East and the South (Fredriksson 1985).

When the sport of rodeo was starting to take form in the 1900s, there were times when workers needed to repair a fence or take an injured cowboy out of the arena, pausing the performance which caused many patrons to leave early. Cowboys, called "clowns," were hired to amuse the audience until the rodeo contest started again. In the 1920s the role of clown came into existence as a full-time activity to fulfill the need for entertainment. Jasbo Fulkersdon, tired of "being run over" by the livestock in the late 1930s, rolled out a protective wooden barrel reinforced on the outside with old car tire casings, creating the barrelman, one of those who helped protect the contestants (Admin 2016, Ordway 2004a, 2004b).

By 1931 rodeo began to be referred to as "a national institution" and "a "big business" (Fredriksson 1985).

The first national cowboys' organization started in 1936, when a group of cowboys and cowgirls boycotted the promoter's rodeo, in Boston Garden. They forced one of the biggest rodeo producers of the times, Col. W.T. Johnson, to listen to their demands for better prize money and judges who understood rodeo. The group named themselves the Cowboys' Turtle Association because they had been slow to act, but had finally stuck their necks out for their cause.

In 1941 the Rodeo Fans of America was formed by Dr. Leo "Two-Gun" Brady, an Edicott, New York, dentist (Fredriksson 1985).

The web page of the Santa Fe, New Mexico rodeo stated

> The Rodeo de Santa Fe began in 1949 when Roy Butler, Austin "Slim" Green, Gene Petchesky, Paul Ragle, Paul Rutledge and few others had a dream and determination to organize a professional rodeo in Santa Fe . . .

In 1945, the Turtles became the Rodeo Cowboys Association (RCA), and then in 1975 became the Professional Rodeo Cowboys Association with headqarters in Colorado Springs, Colorado. In 1979 they opened the ProRodeo Hall of Fame and Museum of the American Cowboy.

By 2013, $39.6 million was paid out in prize money at PRCA. ProRodeo is telecast to more than 50 million households. Rodeo fans keep up to date with their favorite human and animal athletes by subscribing to the PRCA's ProRodeo Sports News magazine and logging on to www.ProRodeo.com, the PSN, and ProRodeo.com use the social networking site.

A cowboy may enter as many as 150 rodeos a year, handle 450 or more animals, and compete for around 90 minutes. Commerical sponsorships of cowboys has become a highly involved business (Fredriksson 1985).

The Professional Rodeo Cowboys Association

A PRCA member spends more than 200 days a year on the road in search of a berth in the Wrangler National Finals Rodeo – the sport's Super Bowl

Each contestant can compete in and out of his circuit throughout the year, but only the points he earns within the circuit from the PRCA circuit system he designates at the beginning of the season are applied toward his place in the circuit standings. However, everything he wins in and out of his chosen circuit is applied toward his world standings. So, while most circuit contestants rodeo close to home, there is still opportunity for them to earn enough money to get to the Wrangler National Finals Rodeo.

The tournament-style NCFR determines the national circuit champions in each event. All 26 qualifiers from the 13 circuits compete in the two preliminary rounds of the rodeo. The top eight contestants overall from each event advance to the semifinal round, with all previous scores and times thrown out. The top four move on to the final round – a sudden-death competition that determines the national circuit champion in each event. Because the top four contestants begin with a clean slate in the final round, each one has an equal opportunity to claim an NCFR title.

The NCFR event winners receive a $20,000 voucher for a new RAM vehicle, a Polaris RANGER UTV, a pair of exotic boots from Justin Boots, a trophy saddle from Cactus Saddlery and a Montana Silversmiths buckle, in addition to their winnings. And the circuit from the PRCA circuit system winning the most money overall at the NCFR retains bragging rights for the year (and a nice bonus from RAM). It is a tournament-style rodeo attended by the top 24 qualifiers per event from the 12 circuits that represent the United States. The RNCFR consists of four preliminary rounds, a semi-final round (with all previous scores thrown out), and a sudden-death final round that determines the national circuit champion of each event.

The Circuits

The Columbia River Circuit has 7 rodeos.
The California Circuit has 36 rodeos.
The Wilderness Circuit has 16 rodeos.
The Montana Circuit has 46 rodeos.
The Mountain States has 11 rodeos.
The Turquoise Circuit has 31 rodeos.
The Badlands Circuit has 12 rodeos.
The Prairie Circuit has 33 rodeos.
The Texas Circuit has 60 rodeos.
The Great Lakes Circuit has 39 rodeos.
The Southwestern Circuit has 60 rodeos.
The First Frontier Circuit has 15 rodeos.

☞ *Citations* ☜

Adams, Samuel Hopkins
  1907 *The Great American Fraud.* 4th Edition. P. F. Collier & Son.

Anderson, Norman D.
  1992 *Ferris Wheels. An Illustrated History.* Bowling Green State University Popular Press: Bowling Green, Ohio.

Admin
  2016 "The Role and Responsibilities of Rodeo Clowns and Barrelmen." In, *Silver Spurs* (June 29).
    https://www.silverspursrodeo.com/oversized -jeans-clown-make-up-and-a-barrel-rodeo -clowns-and-their-role-in-rodeo/

Anon
  n.d.1 *John Robinson Circus.* Circusesandsideshows.com/circuses/johnribo nsoncircus.html
  n.d.2 *Sideshows*

http://www.circusesandsideshows.com/
sideshows.html

n.d.3 "Barnum's Aquarial Gardens (June 1862 – February 1863) in Boston, Massachusetts." In, *WikiVisually*.
https://wikivisually.com/wiki/Barnum%27s _Aquarial_Gardens

n.d. 4 Miller Bros. 101 Ranch Wild West Show .
http://www.circusesandsideshows.com/ circuses/millerbros101.html

n.d. 5 *The Old West on the 101.*
https://sites.rootsweb.com/~okttp/history/101/ 101_ranch_e.htm

1913 "The Month's Rodeo." In, Sunset magazine, Vol. 31

American Engineer

1913 *Railway Age Gazette including the American Engineer.* Issued during the M.M. and M. C. B. Conventions. Vol. 87, page 56.

American Heritage

1966 "The Fat Man And His Friends." Vol. 17, Issue 4 (June).

1974 "Setting The Record Straight On Old Bet." Vol. 25, Issue 3 (April).

Amondson, Christian

2013 "10 Dangerous Drugs Once Marketed as Medicine."

https://www.bestmedicaldegrees.com/10-dangerous-drugs-once
-marketed-as-medicine/

Applebome, Peter
    1989   "Wrangling Over Where Rodeo Began." In, *The New York Times* (June 18).

Ariano, Terry
    2004   "Beasts and Ballyhoo, The Menagerie Men of Somers." Presented by at the Circus Historical Society Annual Meeting. Nyack, New York, July 15.

ASHP American Social History Productions, Inc.
    2002   The Lost Museum. American Social History Project/Center for Media and Learning, The Graduate Center, City University of New York in collaboration with Roy Rosenzweig Center for History and New Media George Mason University. https://lostmuseum.cuny.edu

Baker, Peggy M.
    n.d.   "PATENT MEDICINE: Cures & Quacks." *Pilgrim Society & Pilgrim Hall Museum.*

Barnum, P.T.
    1855   The Autobiography of P. T. Barnum: Clerk, Merchant, Editor and Showman. Ward & Lock: London.

1872 *Struggles and Triumphs: Or, Forty Years' Recollections Of P. T. Barnum.* Written by Himself. Warren, Johnson & Co.: Buffalo, New York.

1888 *The Life of P. T. Barnum: Written by Himself, Including His golden rules For Money Making. Brought Up To 1888.* The Courier Company, Printers: Buffalo, New York.

Baumann, John

1887 "On a Western Ranche." In, *Fortnightly Review,* Vol. 47, New Series (April 1). Chapman and Hall Limited: London. One of the most prominent and influential magazines in nineteenth-century England.

Beale, Paul (editor)

1989 *Partridge's Concise Dictionary of Slang and Unconventional English. The Work of Eric Partridge.* Macmillan Publishing Company: New York.

Beals, Shawn R.

2016 "Coleman's Carnival Opens For Milestone 100th Season In Middletown." In, *Hartford Courant* (Apr 1).
https://www.courant.com/community
/middletown/hc-middletown
-coleman-carnival-100th-year-0331

-20160401-story.html

Beck, Henry Cabot
   2011   "The Legacy of C. B. Irwin and the Y-6 Ranch."
           In, *True West Magazine. History of the American
           Frontier.* (April 26).

Beier, Lucina McCray
   2009   *Health Culture in the Heartland, 1880-1980.*
           University of Illinois.

Benjamin, Ph.D., William, and Barbara Williams
   2016   "Carousel History Feature – American
           Carousel Pioneers – Andrew Christian and
           Charles Dare, Part 1;" "Part 2 – History of The
           New York Carousal Manufacturing Co. – 1889
           to ca. 1898;" "Part 3 – Surviving Carousels,
           Discussion, References, Acknowledgements
           [spelling in original]." In, *Carousel History.*
           CarouselHistory.com. (August 3).

Billboard
   1908   *Circus Gossip* (column). (July 25).
   1945   *Circus Historical Society* (column) (Oct 20).

Bird, Isabella L.
   1875   *The Hawaiian Archipelago.* CreateSpace
           Independent Publishing Platform (October 21,
           2014). Paperback.

Biron, Gerry

    2013   "Iroquois Medicine Men." In, *Whispering Wind Magazine*, Vol 42, No. 1: Folson Louisiana.

Bogdan, Robert

    1988   *Freak Show. Presenting Human Oddities for Amusement and Profit*. University of Chicago Press: Chicago.

Bondeson, Jay

    1999   *The Feejee Mermaid and Other Essays in Natural and Unnatural History*. Cornell University Press.

Bradbury, Joseph T.

    1957   "Circus Wagon History File." In, *Bandwagon*, Vol. 1, No. 4. (Sep-Oct). Circus Historical Society.
        http://classic.circushistory.org/Bandwagon/bw-1957Sep.htm

Brand, Donald D.

    1961   "The Early History of the Rande Cattle Industry in Northern Mexico." *Agricultural History*, Vol. 35, No. 3 (July). Agricultural History Society: Washington, D.C.

Branigan, Jane

    2012   "Charlie Irwin and Cheyenne Frontier Days." (July 12).
        https://naglewarrenmansion.wordpress.com/

Brigham, David R.
1966   "Ask the Beasts, and They Shall Teach Thee:
The Human Lessons of Charles Willson Peale's
Natural History Displays." In, *Huntington
Library Quarterly*, VOL. 59, No. 2/3. University
of Pennsylvania Press.

Britannica
2019   "Minstrel show. American Theatre." Written by
The Editors of the Encyclopaedia Britannica.

https://www.britannica.com/art/minstrel-show#ref1067222

Broadbent, R. J.
1908   *Annals of the Liverpool Stage From the Earliest
Period to the Present Time.* Edward Hall:
Liverpool.

Brown, Col. T. Allison
1994   *Amphitheatres and Circuses: A History from Their
Earliest Date to 1861, with Sketches of Some of the
Principal Performers.* Editor, William L. Borgo
Press: San Bernardino, California.

Brown's Amusements
2020   "Brown's History."
http://brownsamusements.com/pageserver
/history

Brooke, Bob
    2001   "Step Right Up." *History Magazine* (Oct/Nov).

Brown, T. Allison
    2018   *A History of the New York Stage, Vol. 1 of 3: From the First Performance in 1732 to 1901* .(Classic Reprint) Hardcover – January 9, 2018. Original ca. 1888.

Brown, Mary Ann Sachse
    2011   "Codys stand their ground." In, *Leavenworth Times* (September 8). Leavenworth, Kansas. https://www.leavenworthtimes.com/article/20 110908/NEWS/309089835

Burcham, L. T.
    1961   "Cattle and Range Forage in California: 1770-1880." *Agricultural History*, Vol. 35, No. 3 (July). Agricultural History Society: Washington, D.C.

Butchart, Amber
    n.d.   "Fashioning the Freak Show. Orientalism and the Circassian Beauty." In, *Vestoj. The Platform for Critical Thinking on Fashion.* http://vestoj.com/fashioning-the-freak-show/

Butler, Steven Ray
    2006   *Away O'er The Waves: The Transatlantic Life and Literature of Captain Mayne Reid.* Doctor of

Philosophy dissertation. The University of
Texas At Arlington.

Calgary Stampede
    2020   "The Early Years. 1886-1913."
          https://www.calgarystampede.com/heritage
          /history/next-hundred-years

Campy's
    2020   "Campy's Amusements History. It All Started
          In 1969 . . .." In, *Campy's Blue Star Amusements*.
          https://campys.com/pageserver/about-us

Carlson, Paul H.
    2006   *Cowboy Way: An Exploration of History and
          Culture*. Texas Tech University Press.

Carlyon, David
    2001   Dan Rice: The Most Famous Man You've Never
          Heard of. PublicAffairs: New York.

Carnival Warehouse
    2019   "Browns Amusements: an Expanding Carnival
          Route."
          https://carnivalwarehouse.com/newsserver
          /browns-amusements-an-
          expanding-carnival-route-1545955200

Caswell, Estelle
    2017   "Why cartoon characters wear gloves. Those little gloves reveal the fascinating origins of animation." VOX Media.
    https://www.vox.com/videos/2017/2/2/14483952/why-old-cartoons-mickey-mouse-wear-gloves

Chetwynd, Josh
    2012   *How the Hot Dog Found Its Bun: Accidental Discoveries and Unexpected Inspirations That Shape What We Eat and Drink*. Lyons Press: An imprint of Rowman & Littlefield.

Chindahl, George L.
    1959   *A History of the Circus In America*. The Claxton Printers, Ltd.: Caldwell, Idaho.

Circus Historical Society, Inc.
    2020   "Gollmar Bros. Four Mirror Tableau."
    https://www.circuswagons.org/tableaus/gollmar-bros-four-mirror-tableau/

Clayton, John
    2014   "The Old West's Female Champion: Caroline Lockhart and Wyoming's Cowboy Heritage." In, WyoHistory.org. (November 8).
    https://www.wyohistory.org/encyclopedia/old-wests-female-champion-caroline

-lockhart-and-wyomings-cowboy-heritage

Clayton, Lawrence, and Jim Hoy, Jerald Underwood.
    2001   *Vaqueros, Cowboys, and Buckaroos*. University of
          Texas (1st Edition).

Cline, Bob
    2008   "Cummins Wild West - circa 1906 to 1910."
          (July) *Sawdust & Spangles*.
          ircustents.blogspot.com/2008/07/cummins
          -wild-west-circa-1906-to-1910.html

Coaster Guy
    2012   "Ride Profile: Scrambler." In, *The Coaster Guy*
          (August 8).
          http://www.thecoasterguy.com/2012
          /08/08/ride-profile-scrambler/

Cockrell, Dale
    1997   *Demons of Disorder. Early Blackface Minstrels and
          Their World*. Cambridge University Press.

Cody Archive
    n. d.   "Cody, Isaac, 1811-1857." In, *Buffalo Bill Center
          of The West*. William F. Cody Archive.
          Documenting the life and times of Buffalo Bill.
          http://codyarchive.org/life
          /wfc.person.html#cody.i

Cody, Col. William F. (Buffalo Bill).
  1917   *The Adventures of Buffalo Bill*. Harper & Row: New York.

Cole, Jim
  2007   "Meet the Fabulous Flying Pages." In, *Circus 4 Youth*. http://archive.circus4youth.us/res_det.php?res_id=36

Cook, James W.
  2001   *The Arts of Deception. Playing With Fraud in the Age of Barnum*. Harvard University Press: Cambridge, Massachusetts.

Coppedge, Clay
  2018   "Milt Hinkle, the South America Kid and aerial bulldogger." In, *Letters from Central Texas*. (January 13). A column on TexasEscapes.com

Coppock, Mike
  2015   "The Buffalos Hunter's War." In, *True West Magazine. History of the American Frontier* (October).

Costa, Dora
  2015   "Health and the Economy in the United States, from 1750 to the Present." In, *Journal of Economic Literature*, Vol. 53, No. 3 (September).

Coup, William Cameron
    1901   *Sawdust and Spangles. Stories and Secrets of the Circus*. Herbert S. Stone and Company: Eldridge Court, Chicago.

Courtright, William
    1901   *The Complete Minstrel Guide*. The Dramatic Publishing Company.

Crockett, Zachary
    2014   "The Rise and Fall of Circus Freakshows." In, *Priceonomic*. (April) https://priceonomics.com/the-rise-and-fall-of-circus-freakshows/

Culhane, John
    1991   *The American Circus. An Illustrated History*. An Owl Book, Henry Holt and Company: New York.

Dahlinger, Fred Jr.
    1984   "Ringling Bros. Bell Wagon." Circus Wagon History File, Bandwagon, Nov./Dec. circushistory.org/archive/ringling-bros-bell-wagon/

Davis, Lee
    2000   *Scandals and Follies: The Rise and Fall of the Great Broadway Revue*. Limelight Editions: New York.

Davis, Genie

> 2018a "Great Northern Carnival: A Tradition in the Southwest." In, *CarnivalWarehouse* (May 14). https://carnivalwarehouse.com /newsserver/great-northern-carnival-a-tradition-in-the-southwest-1526256000

> 2018b "Frazier Shows holds the line on purchases for 2019. Show makes substantial investment in winter-quarter upgrade." In, *CarnivalWarehouse* (December 17). https://carnivalwarehouse.com /newsserver/frazier-shows-holds-the-line-on-purchases-for-2019-1545004800

> 2020 "James H. Drew Exposition: Unique Rides Draw Strong Attendance in 2019." In, *CarnivalWarehouse* (January 13) https://carnivalwarehouse.com /newsserver/james-h-drew-exposition-unique-rides-draw-strong-attendance -in-2019-1578873600

Day, Cassandra

> 2019 "Coleman carnival set to open for 103rd year — with rain in forecast." In, *The Middletown Press* (Apr 2). https://www.middletownpress.com /middletown/article/Coleman-carnival -set-to-open-for-103rd-year-13735867.php

Dead Media Archive
2010 "Traveling Medicine Show." *NYU- Department of Media, Culture, and Communication.*

DCHS (Dickinson County Historical Society)
2011 "The Amusement King." (February 21). https://dkcohistory.blogspot.com/2011/02 /amusement-king.html

Devlin,Wendy
2020 "Charreada in Guadalajara." In, *MexConnect,* Mexico's top
English-language online magazine, providing quality information about Mexico and promoting Mexico to the world (24 July 2020).

Dewel, Bob
1998 *Sauk County and Baraboo: Volume I.* Baraboo Public Library:Wisconsin

Diab, Khaled
2015 "Circassian beauties and the ugly face of race. The curious case of Rachel Dolezal and the Circassian ladies of yore show just how meaningless the notion of race is." In, *Aljazeera* (25 June). Opinion/Politics.
https://www.aljazeera.com/indepth /opinion/2015/06/circassian-beauties- ugly-face-race-150623073549957.html

Doc's Midway Cookhouse

    2015   "Crafts 20 Big Shows Legacy Comes To An End."
           https://www.docsmidwaycookhouse.com /carnival-history/crafts-20-big-shows/

    2020a "Patent Medicine Shows."
           https://www.docsmidwaycookhouse.com /patent-medicine-shows/

    2020b "Carnival History In America."
           https://www.docsmidwaycookhouse.com /carnival-history/

Dumont, Frank

    1899   *The Witmark Amateur Ministrel Guide and Burnt Cork Encyclopedia*. M. Witmark & Sons: New York.

    1915   "The Younger Generation in Minstrelsy and Reminiscences of the Past." In, the *New York Clipper* (27 March). [a weekly entertainment newspaper 1853-1924].

Elliot, Doug

    2008   "Jumbo the Elephant." *History Magazine* (Feb/Mar).

Ellwanger, Ella Hutchinson

    1919   "Famous Steamboats on Western and Southern Waters." *Register of Kentucky State Historical Society*, Vol. 17, No. 50 (May). Kentucky Historic Society.

Endy, Mary Ann
    2009   "Nonweiler Amusements." In, *Carnival Midway* (November).

Enss, Chris
    2016   "Wild Women Wednesday: Lucille Mulhall." In, *Cowgirl Magazine* (May 11). https://cowgirlmagazine.com /wild-women-wednesday-lucille-mulhall/

FAC
    2015   "About Fantasy. Our History." In, *Fantasy Amusement Company.* https://fantasyamusements.com/?page_id=8

FAHJ
    1913   "Winnipeg Horse Show." In, *Farmers Advocate and Home Journal*, Vol. 48 (June 11).

Farley, Doug
    2008   "ERIE CANAL DISCOVERY: Merchant's Gargling Oil's tie to Lockport." In, *Lockport Union-Sun & Journal Online*, (June 13). https://www.lockportjournal.com /opinion/columns/erie-canal-discovery- merchant-s-gargling-oil-s-tie-to/article _7881f07b-85ce-5a0b-b2ea-22dda2bd7751.html

FatSecret

2007   "Funnel Cake. Nutritional Facts." In, *fatsecret* (21 Aug).
https://www.fatsecret.com
/calories-nutrition/generic/funnel-cake

Feiler, Bruce

2000   "Spun Heaven." In, *Gourmet Magazine* (February).

Felius, Marleen and Marie-Louise Beerling, David S. Buchanan, Bert Theunissen, Peter A. Koolmees, Johannes A. Lenstra

2014   "On the History of Cattle Genetic Resources." *Diversity*, Vol. 6., No 4. (12 November). The journal is a peer-reviewed, open-access journal on the science of biodiversity from molecules, genes, populations, and species, to ecosystems, published monthly online by MDPI.

Find A Grave

2010   "George Fox Bailey." In, *Find A Grave.*
https://www.findagrave.com/memorial
/50503501/george-fox-bailey

Fleming, Candace

2016   *Presenting Buffalo Bill. The Man Who Invented the Wild West.* Roaring Brook Press: New York.

Flynn, Shirley E.
  1996   *Let's Go! Let's Show! Volume One. The History of Cheyenne Frontier Days. The 'Daddy of 'Em All.' "* Wigwam Publishing Company, LLC: Cheyenne, Wyoming.

Fowler, Gene
  2008   *Mavericks: A Gallery of Texas Characters.* University of Texas Press: Austin.

Frazier Shows
  2020   "About Us."
         https://fraziershows.com/pageserver/about-us

Fredriksson, Kristine
  1985   *American Rodeo. From Buffalo Bill to Big Business.* Texas A & M University Press: College Station.

Freese, Kevin
  2018   "The Best is Yet to Come for Tons of Fun Shows was founded in 1991 by Ben's parent, David and Suellen Pfeffer." In, *Midway Magazine* (October).

Frederickson, Mary E.
  2016   "Public Health in the US and Global South." Introduction. - *Southern Spaces.* https://southernspaces.org/2016/public-health -us-and-global-south/

Funtastic

    2017   "Who Invented the Corn Dog?" In, *Funtastic*.
        (August 26).
        https://funtasticshows.com
        /who-invented-the-corn-dog/

Gale, Neil

    2017   *The Midway Plaisance at the 1893 World's*
        Columbian Exposition in Chicago.
        Neil Gale Publishing Company: Belleville,
        Illinois.

Gallagher, John

    2019   "Brown's Amusements keeps the show safe on
        the road." In,
        Freightwaves (July 9).
        https://www.freightwaves.com
        /news/browns-amusements-keeps-the-
        show-safe-on-the-road

GM

    n.d.   "Where Did Funnel Cakes come from?" In,
        Gold Medal
        https://www.gmpopcorn.com
        /resources/blog/where-did-funnel-cakes-
        come-from

Goetzmann, William H., and William N. Goetzmann

    2009   *The West of the Imagination.* 2nd Edition.
        University of Oklahoma Press.

Goodwin, G.G.
    1925   "The First Living Elephant in America." In, *Journal of Mammalogy*, Vol. 6, No. 4 (Nov)

Gossard, Steve (Curator)
    1999   "Jennie Ward." In, *ISU Circus Collection.*

Greatnortherncarnival
    2019   "A Great Northern A'Fair."
           https://greatnortherncarnival.com/

Greenwood, Isaac John (reprinted)
    2015   *The Circus: Its Origin And Growth Prior To 1835, Issues 5-7.* Palala Press: (Originally published in 1898)

Grosvenor, Edwin S., and Robert C. Toll
    2019   "Blackface: the Sad History of Minstrel Shows." In, *American Heritage*, Vol. 64, Issue 1 (Winter). A reprint of Toll's 1978 article, *American Heritage*, (April/May).

Hartsman, Marc
    2005   *American Sideshow. An Encyclopedia of History's Most Wondrous and Curiously Strange Performers.* Jeremy P. Tarcher/Penguin: New York.

GSE

    2020   "About Us." In, *Gopher State Expositions.*
            https://www.gopherstateexpo.com/about-us

Hawkins, Vince

    2014   "The U.S. Army's "Camel Corps" Experiment."
            https://armyhistory.org/the-u-s-armys-camel-
            corps-experiment/(July 16).

HC

    2020   "Amusement Rides – History of the Swing
            Carousels." In, *History of Carousels.*
            http://www.historyofcarousels.com
            /carousel-history/history-of-the-swing
            -carousels/

Hémard, Ned

    2009   "The Floating Palace." New Orleans Nostalgia.
            Remembering New Orleans History, Culture
            and Traditions. *New Orleans Bar Association.*
            Www.neworleansbar.org.

Herda, D. J.

    2019   *The Never-Ending Lives of Liver-Eating Johnson.* A
            Twodot Book: Laham, MD.

Hitchings, A. Frank, and Stephen Willard Phillips

    1906   *Ship Registers of the District of Salem and Beverly,*
            Massachusetts, 1789-1900.
            A. Frank Hitching (copier), Stephen Willard

Phillips (annotations). The Essex Institute: Salem, Massachusetts.

Hoff, James L.
1907 "Status of the Barnum & Bailey Show." *The Billboard* (October 26).

Hoh, Lavahn G.
2004 "The Circus in America: 1793 - 1940". *The Institute for Advanced Technology in the Humanities.* University of Virginia. https://web.archive.org/web/20070331200218/ http://www.circusinamerica.org/public /welcome

Hoh, Lavahn G., and William H. Rough
1990 *Step Right Up. The Adventure of Circus in America.* Betterway Publications, Inc.: White Hall, Virginia.

Holman, Gavin
2017 "Keep it in the Family – the Family Brass Bands that entertained the USA and UK in the late 19th and early 20th centuries." *gavinholman.academia.edu*

Humphreys, Margaret
2009 "How Four Once Common Diseases Were Eliminated From The American South." In, *Health Affairs*, Vol. 28, No. 6. Meeting

HIV/AIDS Costs, Fighting Neglected Disease. (November/December). Bethesda, Mayland.

ICHM (International Circus Hall of Fame)
    n.d.   Glossary of Circus Terminology. Visit.circushallofffame.com

IISM (International Independent Showmen's Museum)
    n.d.   "The History of the Girl Show Goes Way Back To The Mid 1800's."
        https://showmensmuseum.org /exhibits/the-history-of-the-girl-show/
    2013a "Reithoffer Shows 1918 Packard Truck." (January 8).
        showmensmuseum.org /international-independent-showmens -museum-exhibits/reithoffer-shows -1918-packard-truck/
    2013b "Girl Show Revue. The Girl Shows." (October 10).
        https://showmensmuseum.org/exhibits /the-history-of-the-girl-show/
    2015 "Merry Go Round History. The Allan Herschell Company." (March 16).
    2020 "Royal American Shows. WORLD'S LARGEST MIDWAY! Royal American Shows History."
        https://showmensmuseum.org /royal-american-shows/

In Stages
    2016   "JIM CROW'S THEATRICAL ORIGINS." In, *In Stages* (October 21). https://www.instages.org/single-post/2016/10/21/JIM-CROWS-THEATRICAL-ORIGINS

IPC (Inter-state Publishing Company)
    1882   *History of Scott County, Iowa; together with sketches of its cities, villages and townships ... and biographies of representative citizens. History of Iowa Embracing Accounts of the Pre-historic races, aborigines, French, English and American Conquests, and a General Review of Its Civil, Political and Military History.* Inter-State Publishing Co.:Chicago

Jacknis, Ira
    2019   "All the World Is Here: Harvard's Peabody Museum and the Invention of American Anthropology. Exhibit at the Peabody Museum of Archaeology and Ethnology." In, *Museum Anthropology*, V. 42, Issue 2. American Anthropological Association.

Jackson, Bruce
    1967   *The Negro and His Folklore In Nineteenth-Century Periodicals.* University of Texas Press, Austin (for the American Folklore Society).

Jarmes, Glen

n.d. "18,000 See Extravaganza."
http://iagenweb.org/allamakee
/history4/circus.htm

Jensen, Dean

1975 *The Biggest, the Smallest, the Longest, the Shortest. A Chronicle of the American Circus from Its Heartland.* Wisconsin House Book Publishers: Madison, Wisconsin.

Johnson, Dirk

1994 *Biting the Dust. The Wild Ride and Dark Romance of the Rodeo Cowboy and the American West.* Simon & Shuster: New York.

Johnson, E. A.

1953 "William F. Cody, Alias 'Buffalo Bill'." In, *The Annuals of Iowa,* Vol. 32, No. 1 (Summer). State Historical Society of Iowa. Iowas Department of Cultural Affairs.

Johnson, William M.

1990 *The Rose-Tinted Menagerie.* Heretic Books Ltd: London.

Jolly Shows

2020 "The History of Jolly Shows."
https://marylandcarnivals.com
/pageserver/history

Journal News (White Plains, New York)
   1984 "Nathan Howes and the Beginnings of The
         Circus." 26 August (Sunday)

KFF
   n.d. "Funnel Cake and the Festival." In, *Kutztown
         Folk Festival.*
         https://www.kutztownfestival.com
         /press-room/articles/funnel-cake-and-
         festival

Kassel, Mike
   2020 "Angier and the Founding of Cheyenne
         Frontier Days."
         https://www.cfdrodeo.com/cfd-old-west-mus
         eum/our-story/history/
         angier-and-the-founding-of-cheyenne
         -frontier-days/

Kathleen
   2019 "Jump on the Bandwagon...or Circus
         Wagon...or Bandchariot...?" (June 10). *Carriage
         Association of America blog.*
         https://www.carriageassociationofamerica.co
         m/jump-on-the-bandwagon-or-circus-wagon-
         or-bandchariot/

Kaufmann, Helen L.

    1937   *From Jehovah to Jazz.* Dodd, Mead: New York

Kelly, Kate

    n.d.   "First Elephants Brought to the United States."
          America Comes Alive (web page).
    n.d.2 "P.T. Barnum's Early Career." America Comes
          Alive (web page).

Koenig, Dr. Karl

    n.d.   *The History & Music of the Minstrels.*

Kook Science

    2019 "Oregon Indian Medicine Company."
          https://hatch.kookscience.com
          /wiki/Oregon_Indian_Medicine_Company

Kotar, S. L., and J. E. Gessler

    2011 *The Rise of the American Circus, 1716-1899.*
          McFarland & Company, Inc., Publishers:
          Jefferson, North Carolina.

Kudelska, Kamila

    2019 "The Cody Stampede Celebrates 100 Years." In,
          Wyoming Public Media (May 31).
          https://www.wyomingpublicmedia.org
          /post/cody-stampede-celebrates-100-years

Kunhardt, Jr., Philip, and Philip B. Kunhardt III, Peter W. Kunhardt.

> 1995   *P. T. Barnum. America's Greatest Showman.* Alfred A. Knopf: Bew York.

Laegreid, Renee M.

> 2011   "Rodeo Queens." In, *Encyclopedia of the Great Plains.*
> http://plainshumanities.unl.edu /encyclopedia/doc/egp.gen.030.xml

Lahey, Sarah T.

> 2019   "Delavan: Home To Some Of The Greatest Shows." At The Lake. Geneva Lakes Area Magazine. (May 22).
> https://atthelakemagazine.com.

Lajoie, Raymond A.

> 2017   "Joshua C. Stoddard – Inventor of the Steam Calliope." Keyboardmag.com (29 March, updated 29 November).

LeCompte, Mary Lou

> 1982   "The First American Rodeo Never Happened." In, *Journal of Sport History*, Vol. 9, No. 2 (Summer). University of Illinois Press.
> 1985   "The Hispanic Influence on the History of Rodeo, 1823-1922." In, *Journal of Sport History*, Vol. 12, No. 1 (Spring). University of Illinois Press.

1990 "Home on the Range: Women in Professional Rodeo: 1929-1947)." In, *Journal of Sport History*, Vol. 17, No. 3 (Winter). University of Illinois Press.

Lefler, Leah
2019 "Patent Medicine in the 1800's." In, *Owlcation*. A Maven Channel (April 30). https://owlcation.com/humanities /Patent-Medicine-in-the-1800s

Legends of America
2020a "Buffalo Hunters." https://www.legendsofamerica.com /we-buffalohunters/
2020b "Pawnee Bill – Another Wild West Showman." https://www.legendsofamerica.com /we-pawneebilll/

LHMA (Leavenworth Historical Musem Association)
n.d. "C.W. Parker Carousel Museum & Gift Shop." https://www.visitleavenworthks.com /visitors/page/cw-parker-carousel-museum-gift-shop

Long, Jim
1993 "Patent Medicines. Step right up, don't push, plenty of panaceas for everyone." In, *Mother Earth Living* (February/March). https://www.motherearthliving.com

/health-and-wellness/patent-medicines

Lott, Eric
    2013   *Love & Theft: Blackface Minstrelsy And The
            American Working Class (Race And American
            Culture)*, 20th Edition. Oxford University Press.

LPA
    2015   "LPA issues statement to abolish the "m" word
            ." Little People of America.
            https://www.lpaonline.org/the-m-word

Lurie, Edward
    1988   *Louis Agassiz. A Life In Science.* John Hopkins
            University Press: Baltimore.

Made How
    2020   "Ferris Wheel." In, *Made How* (Vol. 6).
            http://www.madehow.com
            /Volume-6/Ferris-Wheel.html

Malanowski, Jamie
    2015   "The Brief History of the Ferris Wheel.
            Originally the American answer to the Eiffel
            Tower, the summertime amusement became a
            hallmark of summer fun." In, *Smithsonian
            Magazine* (June).
            https://www.smithsonianmag.com/history/his
            tory-ferris-wheel
            -180955300/

Mandell, Jonathan

2019   "Blackface on Stage: The Complicated History of Minstrel Shows." In, *New York Theater* (February 7).
https://newyorktheater.me
/2019/02/07/blackface-on-stage-the
-complicated-history-of-minstrel-shows/

Mangan, Gregg

2019   "P. T. Barnum: An Entertaining Life." Connecticut History.org (July 5).

McCubbin, Robert G., and Chriss Enss

2006   "Act One: Buffalo Guys and Gals." In, *The True West Magazine. History of the American Frontier.* (Dec 1).

McLaird, James D.

2005   *Calamity Jane. The Woman and the Legend.* University of Oklahoma Press: Norman

McMurtry, Larry

2005   *The Colonel and Little Missie. Buffalo Bill, Annie Oakley, and the Beginnings of Superstardom in America.* Simon & Schuster: New York.

McNamara, Brooks

1995   *Step Right Up.* Doubleday & Co.: New York.

MacPherson, James
    2008   "Hard times at carnivals knock rides for loop-the-loop. The soaring cost of fuel and shrinking attendance have put squeeze on shows." In, *Chron* (July 3). https://www.chron.com/news /nation-world/article/Hard-times-at-carnivals-knock-rides-for-1781330.php

Merrick, George Byron
    1909   *Old Times on the Upper Mississippi. The Recollections of a Steamboat Pilot from 1854 to1863.* The Arthur H. Clark Company: Cleveland, Ohio.

Meyer V, Ferdinand
    2012   "Merchant's Gargling Oil – 'for Man and Beast'." Peachridge Glass. https://www.peachridgeglass.com/2012 /08/merchants-gargling-oil-good-for-man-and-beast/

Miller, Kenneth L.
    2013   *The American Traveling Carnival.* Millerbooks, Inc.: Chicago.

Minstrelsy
    n.d.   "Minstrel Structure and Iconography." http://exhibits.lib.usf.edu/exhibits/show /minstrelsy/jimcrow-to-jolson

/structure-and-iconography

Miracle, Seana
2015   "The Legacy of Booger Red – The Last of the Rugged Individuals." In, *PPIE100* (May 30). California Historical Society. https://ppie100.org/boogerred/

MNOPEDIA
2019   "Sellner Manufacturing Company." In, MNOPEDIA (June 24). https://www.mnopedia.org/group /sellner-manufacturing-company

Montgomery, David, and Kelly McCullough
2013   "Albert C. Ringling (1852-1916)." In, *Immigrant Entrepreneurship. German-American Business Biographies. 1920 To The Present.* https://www.immigrantentrepreneurship.org /entry.php?rec=168

New England Aquarium
2011   "The South Boston Aquarium (1912 - 1954)." In, New England Aquarium. http://www.neaq.org/about_us /mission_and_vision/aquarium_history /boston_aquarial_and_zoological.php

New England Historical Society
    2019   "The Kickapoo Indian Medicine Company of
            New Haven Entertains the Masses (But Doesn't
            Cure Them)."
            https://www.newenglandhistoricalsociety.com

New York Clipper
    1913   "Oklahoma Ranch Wild West Opens. Passaic,
            N. J., Turns Out and Gives Them A Glorious
            Send-off." In, *New York Clipper. Oldest Theatrical
            Journal in America, Founded in 1853 by Frank
            Queen* (May 3).

New York Daily Times
    1856   "Horrible   Traffic   in   Circassian
            Women—Infanticide in Turkey."In, *The New
            York Daily Times* (August 6)

(NYDM) New York Dramatic Mirror
    1909   Circuses. California Frank's All Star Wild West:
            Philadelphia, PA – Indefinite. (August 7).

New York Times
    1907   "Augustus Ringling Dead. Head of Tented
            Shows in America Dies in New Orleans." In,
            The New York Times (December 19).

NHL

2016   National Hockey League.
www.nhl.com/rangers/team/history-of
-madison-square-garden,
msgnetworks.com/2016/10/13/rangers-first
-opening-night-1926).

Nichols, Max

2010   "Pawnee Bill's Wild West Show plans to keep
the history alive." In, *The Oklahoman,* (Sunday,
May 30).

Nickell, Joe

2005   *Secrets of the Sideshow.* University Press of
Kentucky: Lexington, Kentucky.

19thCenturyLives

2013a   *Cayetano Mariotinit:* The 19th-Century Circus &
Cayetano's Tour. Veronica475 (4 November
2013).

2013b   *Cayetano Mariotinit: Short Time, Big Impact (Part
I).* Veronica474 (21 November 2013)
A collaborative blog authored by students
enrolled in Professor Mary Niall Mitchell's
history courses at the University of New
Orleans. Blog at *WordPress.com.*

Nonweiler

n.d.   Welcome to Nonweiler Amusements.
http://www.nonweileramusements.com/

index.html

North, Henry Ringling, and Alden Hatch
>1960 *The Circus Kings. Our Ringling Family Story.* Doubleday & Company, Inc.: Garden City, New York.

ODB
>n.d. "Stock Characters in Minstrelsy." In, *An Octoroon Dramaturigcal Blog.* https://woollymammothoctoroon.wordpress.com/minstrel-show-stock-characters/

O'Callaghan, Edmund Bailey
>1868 Laws and ordinances of New Netherland, 1638-1674; compiled and translated from the original Dutch records in the office of the secretary of state, Albany, N.Y.

Old Main Artifacts
>2015 "Dr. C. Wakefield & Company, Bloomington, IL." (March 25). Illinois State University. https://oldmainartifacts.wordpress.com/2015/03/26/dr-c-wakefield-company-bloomington-il/

Olson, Jim
>n.d "C. B. Irwin – Larger Than Life." In, *Triple A Livestock Report.* Sponsored by the New Mexico Stockman & Livestock Market Digest:

Albuquerque, New Mexico.
aaalivestock.com/xtra/c-b-irwin-larger-than-life/

2014 "Samuel Thomas Privett - The Legend of
Booger Red." In, *The All-Around* (October).
https://npaper-wehaa.com/all-around/2014/09
/#?article=2336023

Ordway, Kathryn
2004a *Colorado's Rodeo Roots.* B.A. Thesis, Colorado
State University. Denver, Colorado.
2004b *Colorado's Rodeo Roots to Modern-day Cowboys.*
The Donning Company Publishers: Virginia
Beach, Virginia.

Oswald, Alison
2019 "A Swinging Amusement. The Traver Circle
Swing Company, builders of the world's
greatest amusement, brought thrills to the
masses." In, *Lemelson Center for the Study of
Invention and Innovation* (September 20).
https://invention.si.edu/swinging-amusement

Padgett, Ken
n.d. "Blackface! Minstrel Shows."
https://black-face.com/minstrel-shows.htm

Parker, Richard
2015 "Buckskin Bill's Wild West Show." In, *Jackson
Purchase Historical Society*: Vol. 42, No. 1 ,
Article 3. https://digitalcommons

.murraystate.edu/jphs/vol42/iss1/3

Parkinson, Tom
    1956   "Fly Thru the Triple With Greatest Ease." in, *The Billboard* (October 20).

Parks, Shoshi
    2018   "These women were the toughest performers in the Wild West. Don't try horse diving at home." In, *Timeline*. https://timeline.com/women-wild -west-horse-diver-d7e810e7d681

Partridge, Eric
    1961   *A Dictionary of Slang and Unconventional English from the Fifteenth Century to the Present Day*, 5th Edition. The Macmillan Company: New York.

Petersen, William J.
    1970   "Some Diamond Jo Vignettes." In, *The Palimpsest*, Vol. 51, No. 4, Article 5. the State Historical Society of Iowa. Iowa Department of Cultural Affairs.

Polly (Stacey McAdams)
    2019   "Did the Ferris Wheel Originate In New York Not Chicago As Many Believe." *96.9 WOUR* (June 25). Townsquare Media, Inc. https://wour.com/did-the-ferris-wheel -originate-in-new-york-not-chicago

-as-many-believe/

Poole, Andrew
 2011 "Mother Nature didn't rain on Hornell's parade this time around." In, *The Evening Tribune* (Mar 13). New York. https://www.eveningtribune.com /article/20110313/NEWS/303139999

Poppiti, Kimberly
 2018 *A History of Equestrian Drama in the United States: Hippodrama's Pure Air and Fire.* Routledge: New York.

Powell, Tom
 2018 "On The Earie by Tom Powell, OABA News Ambassador." In, *OABA*, Outdoor Amusement Business Association (May 16). https://www.oaba.org/news/7344708

Pursell, Carroll
 2015 *From Playgrounds to Playstation. The Interaction of Technology and Play.* John Hopkins University Press: Baltimore.

Pyle, Jinx, and Jayne Peace
 2004 "Rodeo 101. History of the Payson Arizona Rodeo 1884-1984."

Raish, Carol and Aline McSweeny
2001   "Livestock Ranching and Traditional Culture in Northern New Mexico." In, *Natural Resources Journal*, Vol. 41, No. 3 (Summer). University of New Mexico School of Law: Albuquerque, New Mexico.

Rawson, Hugh
1989   *Wicked Words. A Treasury of Curses, Insults, Put-Downs, and Other Formerly Unprintable Terms from Anglo-Saxon Times to the Present.* Crown Publishers: New York.

Reid, Rebecca N.
2010   *"Flirting and Boisterous Conduct Prohibited": Women's Work In Wisconsin Circuses: 1890-1930.* Bachelor of Arts Thesis, Department of History. The University of Wisconsin: Eau Claire, Wisconsin.

Reiss, Benjamin.
1999   "P.T. Barnum, Joice Heth and Antebellum Spectacles of Race." In, *American Quarterly*, Vol.51, No. 1 (March).

Reithoffer
2020   "Family Run Family Fun Since 1896! Hard work and sacrifice - How our family has lived the American Dream for 5 generations." In, *Reithoffer Shows.*

https://www.reithoffershows.com/history/

Religious Telescope
    1903   "Current News." In, *Religious News*, Vol. 69.

Rhodes, Cynthia K.
    2010   *Lucille Mulhall: An Athlete of Her Time*. Eloquent Books: New York.

RJD (The Record Journal of Douglas County)
    1951   "Cincinnati Trapshooter Invented First 'Clay' Pigeon 70 Years Ago." In, *The Record Journal of Douglas County* (January 5). Castle Rock, Colorado. https://www.coloradohistoricnewspapers.org/

Rogers, Will
    1996   *The Papers of Will Rogers. The Early Years. Volume 1. November 1879 - April 1904.* Arthur Frank Wertheim and Barbara Bair (editors). University of Oklahoma Press: Norman.
    2000   *The Papers of Will Rogers. Wild West and Vaudeville. Volume Two. April 1904 - September 1908.* Arthur Frank Wertheim and Barbara Bair (editors). University of Oklahoma Press: Norman.

Rookmaaker, L.C.
    1998   *The Rhinoceros in Captivity.* Kugler Publications:
           Amsterdam

Russell, Carol L., and Thomas E. Murray
    2004   "The Life and Death of Carnie." In, *American*
           Speech, Vol. 79, No. 4. Duke University Press.

Sacramento Union
    1914   "Wild West Show Coming. Irwin Brothers Will
           Be Here Soon." Vol. 177, No. 19 (19 July).

Sagan, Carl
    1997   *The Demon-Haunted World. Science As A Candle*
           in the Dark. Ballantine Books: New York.

Sampson, Henry T.
    2014   *Blacks in Blackface: A Sourcebook on Early Black*
           Musical Shows. Scarecrow Press, Inc,.: Lanham,
           Maryland.

Savitt, Todd L., and James Harvey Young (Editers)
    1988   *Disease and Distinctiveness in the American South.*
           The University of Tennessee Press: Knoxville.

Schramm, Henry
    1839   *Empire Showcase: A History of the New York State*
           Fair. North Country Books.

Scott, Frank

1987   "First Cowgirl' Raised in Oklahoma." In, *The Oklahoman* (Nov 15). https://oklahoman.com/article/2205631 /first-cowgirl-raised-in-oklahoma

Scripophily

n.d.   "Barnum & Bailey Limited (Issued to The Commercial Bank of Scotland) 1902. RARE." https://scripophily.net/barbaillim19.html

Scofield, Rebessa Elena

2015   *Riding Bareback: Rodeo Communities and the Construction of American Gender, Sexuality, and Race in the Twentieth Century.* Doctoral dissertation. Harvard University, Graduate School of Arts & Sciences.

Shaw, B. Derek

2019   "Chance's Zipper, 50 years of thrills for a king of the midway." In, *Amusement Today* (June).

Showmen's Museum

2014   "Minstrel Show History." (December 28). https://showmensmuseum.org /international-independent-showmens- museum-exhibits/minstrel-show-exhibit/

SHUOA

    n.d.   Skyline House - The History of Bailey's Crossroads
          www.shuoa.org/community/historybaileys.html

Siciliano-Rosen, Laura

    n.d.   "Funnel Cake." In, *Britannica*.
          https://www.britannica.com/topic/funnel-cake

Sideshow World

    n.d.   "Oregon Indian Medicine Company."
          http://www.sideshowworld.com/43-SO-MS/Oregon/Indian-Med-Show.html

Simmons, Marc

    2016   "Why early New Mexico turned from cattle to sheep." (April 15).
          antafenewmexican.com/news/local_news/why-early-new-mexico-turned-from-cattle-to-sheep/article_a70446e1-d775-5be5-afaa-34a3e7c811e5.html

Simmons, R. Laurie; and Thomas H. Simmons

    2016   *Historic Context: The Instant City — The Gold Rush and Early Settlement, 1858-1892.* discoverdenver.com (October 28).

Slout, Willam L.

    1997   *Clowns and Cannons: The American Circus During the Civil War.* Wildside Press LLC: Cabin John,

Maryland.

2000 *A Royal Coupling. The Historic Marriage of Barnum and Bailey.* An Emeritus Enterprise Book: San Bernardino, California.

2010 *Olympians of the Sawdust Circle. A Bibliographical Dictionary of the Nineteenth Century of American Circus.* The Borgo Press: San Bernardino, California.

Smith, Ian

2016 "Rare photos show the Travelling Carnival and fairground scenes of a bygone era." In, *The Vintage News* (March 16).
https://www.thevintagenews.com/2016/03/16/rare-photos-show-travelling-carnival-fairground-scenes-bygone-era/

Solem, Børge

1997 "Nice To Know - Things About Ships." Norwayheritage.com.

Somers Historical Society

N.D. Town of Somers History: Beasts and Ballyhoo, The Menagerie Men of Somers.
http://www.somershistoricalsoc.org/menageries2p6.html

Sotiropoulos, Karen
    2006   *Staging Race. Black Performers in Turn of the Century America.* Harvard University Press. Cambridge.

SS
    2020   "History." In, *Stipe Shows.*
           http://www.stipeshows.com/history.html
           http://www.stipeshows.com/about.html

Stencell, A. W.
    1999   "Shebas On Trampled Grass. Cooch Shows on the Midway.". In, *Girl Show: Into the Canvas World of Bump and Grind.* EWC Press: Toronto, Ontario, Canada.

Strates Shows, Inc.
    n.d.   "Carnival History."
           http://www.stratescarnivalcompany
           .com/history

Steinbacher, Bill
    2008   "Wakefield's Black Berry Balsam. Wakefield's Almanac guaranteed to cure all." (Feb 4). (Steinbacher – KempLibrarian /ArchivistMcLean County Museum of History). http://wakefieldgenealogy.blogspot.com /2008/02/wakefields-blackberry-balsam.html

St Leon, Mark

    2014   "Novel Routes: Circus in the Pacific, 1841-1941." *Popular Entertainment Studies,* Vol. 5, Issue 2. The School of Creative Arts, Faculty of Education & Arts: The University of Newcastle, Australia.

Summers, Candace

    2018   "Noble, Clyde Van." In, Research/Biographies/Noble, Clyde Van. *McLean County Museum of History.* https://www.mchistory.org/research/biographies/noble-clyde-van

SVR (Sun Valley Rides)

    2020   "History of the Mattfeldt Family." https://www.sunvalleyrides.com/history/

TFS

    n.d.   "History of Tons of Fun Shows." In, *Welcome to Tons of Fun Shows.* http://www.tonsoffunshows.com/

Thayer, Stuart

    2005   *American Circus Anthology, Essays of the Early Years.* Arranged and edited by William L. Slout.

THC
2013   "1893: The Lion that Had New York City in an Uproar." In, *The Hatching Cat*. (21 April). http://hatchingcatnyc.com/2013 /04/21/1893-the-lion-uproar/

THS (Trapshooting Hall of Fame)
2020   "George Ligowsky. Hall of Fame Inductee (1969)". https://www.traphof.org/inductees /details/1/89-ligowsky-george

The Lost Museum Archive
2020   "The Joice Heth Exhibit." In, *The Lost Museum Archive*. American Social History Productions, Inc. https://lostmuseum.cuny.edu /archive/exhibit/heth/

The Nation
1865   "A Word About Museums." In, *The Nation*, July 27.
1865   "Mr. Barnum on Museums." In, *The Nation*, August 10.

Thornber, Craig
n.d.   *History of Medicine. Glossary of Medical Terms Used in the 18th and 19th Centuries*. Cheshire, England. https://www.thornber.net/

Toll, Robert C.

1978   "Blackface: the Sad History of Minstrel Shows."
In, *American Heritage* (April/May).

TOM (The Old Motor)

2013   "Armitage-Herschell Company, the
Herschell-Spillman Company and
Herschell-Spillman Engines." In, *The Old Motor*
(May 30). An
comprehensive vintage automobile magazine,
updated daily, published in Brattleboro,
Vermont.
http://theoldmotor.com/?p=82237.

Tracy, Joseph L.

1947   "Chang & Eng." In, *Hobby-Swapper. The
Collector's Monthly* (M ay).

Traffic Bulletin

1913   "Circus Movements." Vol. 2, page 6 (July 12).

Trainor, Sean

2015   "Lessons of the Bearded Lady. Madame
Clofullia was judged by what she said, not how
she looked." In, *The Atlantic* (December).
https://www.theatlantic.com/national/archive
/2015/12/lessons-of-the-bearded-lady/418038/

Trav, S. D.

    2012   "The Lucasies, Family of Albinos." In, *Travalanceche* (webpage). https://travsd.wordpress.com/2012 /12/10/the-lucasies-family-of-albinos/

    2020   "Bryant's Minstrels." In, *Travalanceche* (webpage) (23 February). https://travsd.wordpress.com/2020 /02/23/bryants-minstrels/

Untiedt, Kenneth L.

    2013   *Cowboys, Cops, Killers, and Ghosts: Legends and Lore in Texas*. University of North Texas Press: Denton, Texas.

US

    n.d.   "Frank Charles Bostock (1866-1912). In, *National Fairground and Circus Archive*. University of Sheffield: UK. https://www.sheffield.ac.uk/nfca /projects/frankbostockbio

USF

    n.d1   "African American Minstrel Performers." University of South Florida.

    n.d2   "Minstrel Structure and Iconography." University of Southern Florida.

    n.d3   "Blackface."

    n.d4   "Plantation Nostalgia."

https://exhibits.lib.usf.edu/exhibits/show
/minstrelsy/jimcrow-to-jolson
/african-american-performers

USM (University of Southern Mississippi)
1924 "Circus, Minstrel and Traveling Show Collection." Historical Manuscripts Home. University of South Mississippi. McCain Library and Archives.
https://lib.usm.edu/spcol/collections
/manuscripts/finding_aids/m329.html

Vail, R. W. G.
1933 "Random Notes on The History of The Early American Circus." In, *American Antiquarian Society* [April].
1945 "This Way To The Big Top." In, *New York Historical Society Quarterly*, Vol. 29, No. 3 (July).

Victor, Josh
2017 "History of Carnival Games" (April 12) https://ourpastimes.com/history-carnival-games-10047456.html

Wall, Duncan
2013 *The Ordinary Acrobat. A Journey into the Wondrous World of the Circus, Past and Present.* Alfred A. Knopf: New York

Wallace, Irving
    N. D. P.T. Barnum. American Showman.
    https://www.britannica.com
    /biography/P-T-Barnum

Wallis, Michael
    1999 *The Real Wild West: The 1010 Ranch and the Creation of the American West.* St. Martin's Griffin: New York:

Warren, Louis S.
    2005 *Buffalo Bill's America. William Cody and The Wild West Show.* Vintage: Visalia, California.

Watertown Historical Society
    2020 "Circuses."
    http://www.watertownhistory.org
    /Articles/Circuses.htm

Watkins, Mel
    1994 *On The Real Side. Laughing, Lying, and Signifying – The Underground Tradition of African-American Humor That Transformed American Culture From Slavery to Richard Prior.* Touchstone. Simon & Schuster, Inc.: New York.

Weiser, Kathy
    2017 "Patent Medicine & the Popular Medicine Show."

https://www.legendsofamerica.com
/ah-patentmedicine/

West, Mark Irwin
   1981 "A Spectrum of Spectators: Circus Audiences in Nineteenth-Century America." In, *Journal of Social History*, 15, No. 2. (December).

Westchester County
   N.D. Historical Treasures of Westchester County. Virtual Archives.
   https://www.westchesterarchives.com/HT /muni/wchs/zoological.html

Westerntrips
   2014 "A Little Known Wild West Show / Buckskin Bill's." In, *Western Trips. Historic Stories of the Western U.S. and Low Cost Travel Ideas.* Westerntrips.blogspot.com.

Wiki
   2015 "Wade Shows." In, *Wikipedia.*
   https://en.wikipedia.org/wiki/Wade_Shows
   2019 "Moses Kimball." In, *Wikipedia.*
   https://en.wikipedia.org/wiki/Moses_Kimball
   2020a "Scrambler (ride)." In, *Wikipedia.*
   https://en.wikipedia.org/wiki/Scrambler_(ride)
   2020b "Fiji Mermaid." In, *Wikipedia.*
   https://en.wikipedia.org/wiki/Fiji_mermaid

Willard, John
    2001   "Circus Wonder Wagon." *in, Quad-City Times,* (Aug 28).

Williams, Edgar
    2017   *Hipopotamus.* Reaktion Books: Islington, London, England.

Williams, Greg
    2009   *The French Assault on American Shipping, 1793-1813: a history and comprehensive record of merchant marine losses.* McFarland & Company, Inc., Publishers: Jefferson, North Carolina.

Williams, Sybil R.
    2020   "The American Minstrelsy: Remembering Africa, Birthing America." In, *Signature Theatre.* Arlington, Virginia.

Wilson, Dennis A.
    2012   "A Grant County Circus." in, *History and Politics.* (February 28). https://dennis1950.blogspot.com/2012/02/grant-county-circus.html

Wittmann, Matthew
    2012   "The Transnational History of the Early American Circus." In, *The American Circus.* Edited by Weber, Susan Weber, Kenneth L. Ames, and Matthew Wittmann. Yale University

Press: Bard Graduate Center: Decorative Arts, Design History, Material Culture, New York.

Wohlforth, Charles
  2019 "She ran away with the carnival — and built a unique Alaska life." In, *Anchorage Daily New* (January 6).

Wonning, Paul R.
  2019 *The Agricultural and 4-H Fair-Southeast Edition.* Mossy Feet Books.

World Press
  2018 "Jefferson County Jayhawkers and Forgotten Freestaters."
         In, *Worldpress.com* (January 29).
         https://jeffersonjayhawkers.com/2018/01/

Wolman, David, and Julian Smith
  2019 *Aloha Rodeo. Three Hawaiian Cowboys, The Worlds Greatest Rodeo, and A Hidden History of the American West.* William Morrow: New York .

Wormser, Richard
  2003 *The Rise and Fall of Jim Crow.* St. Martin's Press: New York. York County History Center
  2015 "John Durang; Forming America On Stage."

Young, James Harvey
    1960   "Patent Medicines: An Early Example of Competitive Marketing." In, *The Journal of Economic History,* Vol. 20, No. 4 (Dec). Cambridge University Press.

About The Author

George R. Mead began to study anthropology in 1962 after being discharged (honorably) from the U. S. Army, Combat Engineers. He eventually received a B.A., M. A., and Ph. D. in his chosen field. And many years later an M. S. W. in Clinical Social Work. He was worked in aerospace, taught at the college and university levels, worked in a community action agency, ran a restaurant, been unemployed, and worked for the U. S. Forest Service, and temporally as a door knocking Census worker. He is now retired from the work-a-day world but does a certain amount of consulting, writing, and research. He lives seven miles outside of the small town of La Grande, Oregon, with his wife, one cat, and a Black Lab dog named Jettz who firmly believes that staring into his face at nine-o-clock in the evening is a statement that popcorn should be made.

Made in the USA
Middletown, DE
14 January 2021